PRACTICAL SUGGESTIONS FOR TEACHING

Edited by ALICE MIEL

Observing and Recording the Behavior
of Young Children

TITLES IN THIS SERIES

Observing and Recording

the Behavior of Young Children

DOROTHY H. COHEN
GRADUATE PROGRAMS
BANK STREET COLLEGE OF EDUCATION

VIRGINIA STERN
RESEARCH ASSOCIATE
BANK STREET COLLEGE OF EDUCATION

Teachers College Press

TEACHERS COLLEGE COLUMBIA UNIVERSITY

NEW YORK

FIFTH PRINTING, 1965

© 1958 BY TEACHERS COLLEGE, COLUMBIA UNIVERSITY

LIBRARY OF CONGRESS CATALOG CARD NUMBER: 58–59985

MANUFACTURED IN THE UNITED STATES OF AMERICA

EDITOR'S FOREWORD

READING this pamphlet by Mrs. Cohen and Mrs. Stern is like observing for several months in nursery schools and kindergartens with the added advantage of having at one's side experts to point out the great amount of information being revealed by the children through their movements and their vocalization. These authors help the reader to see the children thinking and socializing with their hands—and their feet! No parent or teacher of younger or older children will be very likely to follow the characters introduced in these pages without forever after seeing with new eyes the struggles and successes experienced by the human being in growing up.

Not every one who attempts to record his observations of children can hope to be as successful as these authors in capturing in words the essence of children's interactions. Perhaps it takes a special flair for writing as well as a special gift for empathizing with a child to write a description like this:

When he is happy, Lee is happy from head to toe. His eyes dance, he roars with laughter, and quivers with delight. He sparkles long after the experience has ended . . .

But those responsible for teaching young children will surely be influenced by this booklet to try to see children and write about them in terms of the "*quality* of their interrelatedness with people and materials." The reader will be impressed with the importance of recording significant information about children and, particularly in the brief section on "Language as a Tool in Recording," will receive practical help in "joggling his memory for verbs, adverbs, adjectives, and phrases that can be used descriptively" in painting a more accurate picture of a flesh-and-blood child.

The pamphlet is carefully built to give help on the details of observing and recording without ever losing the living human being described.   To end with Lee as a whole little boy is to have an ingeniously interesting and useful final demonstration of the recording technique being advocated throughout.

ALICE MIEL

ACKNOWLEDGMENTS

THIS work owes its existence to many more people than the authors alone. We are especially thankful to Louis Cohen for his persistently loyal encouragement and help; to Dr. Millie Almy of Teachers College, Columbia, for her ready understanding of what we were trying to do, and her faith in our ability to do it; and to the many teachers who served willingly in testing the suggestions for recording and generously allowed us to use their results as illustrations in the manual. We want to pay tribute, too, to the late Muriel Ward, whose leadership among New Jersey nursery school teachers stimulated interest in and support of the courses in Observation and Record-taking out of which this manual grew; and to Monema Kenyon, Assistant in Early Childhood in the New Jersey State Department of Education, for her part in bringing these courses into being at Rutgers University.

DOROTHY H. COHEN
VIRGINIA STERN

April 24, 1958

CONTENTS

1

WHY RECORDS?

EACH of us has known at some time the glow of satisfaction that comes with reaching through successfully to a child. Having applied just the right touch at the right moment, we have warmed to the smile of pleasure and trust a child bestows on us when we have understood what he feels and thinks. And each of us has known, too, the frustration of using to no avail tested wiles and approaches, of being baffled and irritated because we have felt completely ineffective with some children. All teachers want to understand their children better. Many have tried to keep records of children's behavior in an effort to gain insight into why they do what they do. But all too often even records conscientiously kept seem to reveal very little, and we fall back on our hunches and our intuition as bases for judgment.

This manual on record-taking describes recording techniques that will help teachers of young children toward their goal of understanding children's behavior. The manual does not tell how to interpret behavior, but it does suggest the details to look for that will be meaningful in explaining behavior. The manual tells how to gather data and how to make the best use of data. It discusses principles of observation rather than principles of diagnosis. If we could say that understanding a child is like unraveling a mystery, then taking records is the gathering of clues. Like experienced detectives we must recognize the significant clues, we must develop special skills.

Teachers of young children do not get very far when they ask children to explain themselves. Nor can they use the personality tests and questionnaires that help in understanding older children. For the present, our best technique seems to be the careful gathering of evidence via the on-the-spot record. To the writers, this means recording details that not only describe the action but reveal how a child feels

1

about what he is doing; details on *how* he does something as well as when; the *quality* as well as the quantity of his interrelating with people and materials; and, of course, what he says.

The most complete recording of this kind, but not necessarily the best for our purposes, would be done by someone who knows shorthand and is not responsible for the life of the group. Obviously it is impossible for teachers to achieve near-perfect written records of all the details they actually see. Nevertheless, there is benefit to be gained from an awareness of what to look for in those odd moments when a teacher can whip out a small pad and let her pencil fly. Every teacher can get some records, and over the months even occasional jottings add up to something impressive! More important is the fact that knowing what is significant makes one generally more aware of the nuances of children's behavior, even if it is not always possible to write things down.

A Teacher Needs to Be One Part Scientist

In suggesting that teachers study children by careful observation and recording of behavior, we are borrowing from research a tool that has aimed at achieving the utmost objectivity and dispassionateness. For teachers observing the children with whom they work and live, absolute objectivity is impossible, and objectivity itself becomes a relative thing. As a matter of fact, it is to be hoped that no teacher would ever try for so much objectivity that she would cease to be a responsible and responsive adult to her group. It is far better for a child to have a warmly interested teacher who has kept no records, than a meticulous observer with no warmth! But if we do not strive for the kind of absolute objectivity that eliminates all feeling, we do seek awareness on the part of the teacher of the kinds of personal, subjective feelings that tend to color records. The picture of a child which is influenced by such teacher involvement might not be true of the child at all.

Suppose we look at a child with this in mind.

Here is Johnny. He is five. He lives on Third Street. He comes to school every day. To Teacher A he is a lovable roughneck, sturdy and full of fun. To Teacher B he is a sloppy child, wild and undisciplined. For Teacher C he hardly exists. To Teacher D he is one big appeal for mothering. Which Johnny is the real Johnny? Does anyone know what Johnny thinks about himself?

Apparently people do not see children with unbiased eyes, or everybody would see the same Johnny. We need to examine these biases, or personal involvements, if we are to have some degree of accuracy in our record-taking.

Our Conception of What Children Should Be Like

When we ourselves were the butt of adult directions, we were told in definite terms what behavior would be tolerated and what would be punished. Within our families, within our communities, there were traditions and opinions, standards and values, set up as guides for our youthful consciences. To be clean was virtuous, to be dirty was naughty. To be polite was to merit love, to be rude brought on a spanking. But family goals were not always the same. Sobriety and thrift formed a code for some people, conviviality and relaxation as serious a code for others. To become a scholar was the goal for some, financial success for others.

When we are little, the teachings of the important adults are impressive. So impressive do they remain, in fact, that when we become adults and teach children in turn, we fall back with greater security and a sense of rightness on what our parents taught us about how children *should* behave than on what psychology tells us about how they *do* behave. That is why Johnny's sloppiness stands out for Teacher B and his good humor for Teacher A. Teacher C can hardly admit that such creatures as Johnny exist because to her way of thinking little boys are just not as nice as little girls! But Teacher D forgives all precisely because he is such a little boy.

If we were to measure fluid milk in pounds and potatoes in quarts, we would be more accurate than if we measured children's behavior in terms of adult virtues and aspirations. While children will, when adult, take on adult ways of behavior, as children they are governed by somewhat different laws that are peculiar to this stage in the life of a human being. We know that a caterpillar is a stage in the life of a moth and it cannot fly. We know that a calf cannot give milk, although some day it will. But all too many people expect the human child to behave as adult as possible, and the sooner the better! In point of fact, we can be much more successful in guiding a child toward mature adulthood if we are clear about the nature of childhood.

Perhaps the thing that fools us about young children is the fact that they can speak. Because this special human ability is achieved so early in life, it is easy to assume that the thinking that lies behind the speech is surely the same as ours. By this reliance on the child's speech as the key to understanding him, we close off too many meaningful avenues of communication between children and ourselves.

How many times do we say to a child, in anger or in sorrow, with insistence or with sweetness, "Why did you do it?" And in anger or in sorrow, belligerently or helplessly, the child answers, "I DON'T KNOW." The truth of the matter is that children do not know, and cannot tell us why they do as they do. When we don't know either, that leaves us both confused!

Children Reveal Themselves in Special Children's Ways

There are reasons for a child's behavior, of course, plenty of them. Sometimes it is hard to decide which is the most likely of several possible reasons for the same kind of behavior! But while every bit of behavior is caused by something, we must sadly admit that what that something is for the particular child who is the enigma is often a mystery. That is why as teachers we must gather good clues that will lead to understanding. Only by learning to see children as they are, and especially as *they see themselves,* will we get our clues. It is not as simple as it sounds.

Young children are still operating out of strong physical and emotional bases. Their bodies not only move into pretzel shapes with fluidity; body movement, body processes, and feelings loom large on the horizon of their existence. Young children *think* with their *hands* (they *touch* to find out) and *socialize* with their *feet* (stamping and kicking noisily are fine acts of comradeship!). Or, they might think with their *feet* (what happens to a worm?) and socialize with their *hands* (what will happen if I touch him in the eye?). If we would record their growing and learning, we must record what they do with their bodies, even as we listen to what they say with their mouths. And we must listen without our grandmother's prejudices peering over our shoulder!

Thus, even though the speech of a young child is a wonderful thing indeed when it occurs, it is far from complete for a long time for all the help it is to adults trying to understand childhood meanings. It is not too good a tool for expressing feelings and thoughts, for example, although it fast becomes highly skilled at expressing *wants.*

(Even that is not true of all children.) Does a young child say, "I feel sad," or does he hang his head, cry, or stare into space (all *physical* expressions)? If we wait for him to grow to the stage where he is mature enough to pinpoint his emotions and tell us about them, we shall wait a long time indeed! We must learn, therefore, to recognize other behavior as clues to thought and feeling.

Children communicate with us through their eyes, the quality of their voices, their body postures, their gestures, their mannerisms, their smiles, their jumping up and down, their listlessness. They show us, by the way they do things as well as by what they do, what is going on inside them. When we have come to see children's behavior through the eyes of its meaning to them, *from the inside out,* we shall be well on our way to understanding them. Recording their ways of communicating helps us to see them as they are.

2

THE ON-THE-SPOT RUNNING RECORD

There Are Many Kinds of Records

THERE are many ways of keeping records of children's behavior to suit different purposes and situations. Some records are frankly *impressionistic* and this is perfectly acceptable at times. When a new child enters school, a teacher cannot help but react to him and size him up in her own terms. If she writes down her impressions, she will have a record to turn to later when she has developed another perspective on the child. How correct are her early impressions? To what extent are they borne out by more knowledge?

Some teachers keep a *log* or *diary* about their group. At the end of the day, or perhaps during rest hour, they put down what stood out that day in as much detail as they have time and energy for. This is an excellent way of recording the activity of the group, its shifts in leadership, its ideas and interests, its accomplishments. It is an invaluable aid to planning. Some teachers do the same thing but with less regularity and only from time to time, spot-checking in a sense. There are charts and checklists that help a teacher remember which children have not used paints for a while, which should get a turn at the workbench, and which are taking a large share of social responsibility. And of course there are snapshots and drawings, movies and tape-recordings (too expensive for most of us!). One can also keep track of the number of times a certain kind of behavior took place, like how many times Jill hit anyone, and how many times she threatened to hit but didn't; or with whom and with what Judy was playing at 10:30 every day during a three-week period. All these techniques are good and can be used profitably. The use of any recording technique, however, must be determined by our purposes.

What are we after? Why are we taking records?

We are here suggesting a recording technique that will show a fairly full and realistic picture of one living, breathing child, as he responds to life in his own unique way, as he interacts with people and materials and functions at his own stage of maturity and growth. It is hard to focus on a child as an individual in this manner when one has grown accustomed to planning for an entire group. But while a group has its own laws of interaction that are surely worth studying, the study of individuals in the group leads to greater awareness of what is significant in human growth and development. The technique of studying one child in detail leads to deeper understanding of the one child and broader knowledge of all children.

Records, however, are not a panacea. They are no more than a means by which a busy teacher can take hold of a squirming, slippery, smiling, screeching, intriguing, and bewildering child and hold him still long enough to examine him carefully. This procedure, taking on-the-spot records of behavior as it is occurring, the authors, for want of a better name, call . . .

. . . The Running Record

It is comforting to know that there are practically no fixed rules in this job of record-taking. The whole technique is relatively new to education; it has its creative aspects and its weaknesses. There will undoubtedly be modifications and changes as the technique becomes more widely used. We are going to be suggestive for the most part, and the rest is up to you!

Since your primary responsibility is to be the teacher of the group, your times for recording will literally have to be snatched. Children's needs come first, and you may have to drop your pencil to race to someone's rescue. It helps to have pads, cards, or a small notebook in all your smock pockets, on shelves around the room, and up your sleeve too. Never miss out on a choice bit because no pencil is handy! Be casual and unobtrusive about it all. Get close enough to hear things, but not so close that you interfere with the play. Notes can be rough and full of abbreviations, to be filled in and cleaned up later. Get the date down and the child's name as well as where the action is set. Should the children ask you what you are doing, don't let them in on the secret because they may become self-conscious. Be nonchalant and say something noncommittal, like "It's teacher's work," or "It's writing I have to do."

Take records of a child at as many different periods of the day as possible, although not necessarily all in one day. You will want to record his behavior at arrival and dismissal, at toileting and at rhythms, at wash-up and at story time, at free play and with creative materials. You will want to see what he does indoors and out, by himself and with others. Recording in a variety of situations will show up all-pervasive behavior, such as relationships with children and adults, adjustment to school, feelings about routines, position in the group, etc.

Often it will seem that these everyday records are not getting any-where, and it is easy to become discouraged. But when, after a period of time, details of similar character are grouped together, patterns of behavior emerge, and we begin to see what it is a child is really doing. Be patient and let the thing grow. Recording behavior is, after all, recording growth, and since children are in transition between stages much of the time, you will need many stills before you see the common movement running throughout.

A Word of Caution

Never, never allow records to lie around in public view. Treat them the way a doctor treats his findings. Even the most inconsequential information about a patient is kept confidential, and we must do the same. Unless there is a professional reason for doing so, tell your funny and delightful stories about children *without identifying the particular child or family.*

3

RECORDING A CHILD'S BEHAVIOR
DURING ROUTINES

Organizing the Information

SINCE we need a starting point, let us start with observing a child at tasks and behavior that make up so much a part of a young child's life—the routines. At school we generally think of these as clean-up, toileting, snack-time, lunch, rest, etc. These are the "uncreative" but necessary aspects of the program that are repeated day after day, the activities around which many a program revolves. Let us look at a child about to become involved in a routine—for example, getting dressed for outdoors. Although this seems to be a simple and obvious activity, let us look at a child with the following questions in mind:

WHAT IS THE STIMULUS FOR THE ACTIVITY?

How does it happen that the child is dressing now?
Did the teacher ask him to, individually?
Did the teacher make an announcement to the class?
Did the child notice others and follow suit?
Did he just get an impulse and begin to dress himself?

In a word, we want to know what set the child off on the dressing process. We could call this spur to action the *stimulus*. It might come from within or outside the child. It might be obvious (the teacher told him to get dressed) or not obvious at all (apparently an unexplained impulse).

WHAT IS THE SETTING?

What's going on around the child while he is dressing?
What is the physical setup affecting the activity? (cubbies or lockers are near or far away, there are chairs to sit on, children crowd into small space, etc.)

Who are the significant people nearby and what are they doing?
(adults who are important to the child, his friends and
enemies, a visitor about whom he is concerned, etc.)

This enveloping activity would be the *setting* in which the behavior
takes place, since obviously nothing happens in a vacuum.

WHAT SEEM TO BE THE CHILD'S REACTIONS?

If the activity was teacher-initiated, how does the child react?
Does he accept the idea?
(willingly? cheerfully? with annoyance? with complaints?
silently?)
Does he resist the idea?
(openly and directly? indirectly?)
If the action seems child-directed, how is it carried out?
(eagerly? stealthily? hastily? calmly? dreamily?)
Does the child show any special attachment to his clothing?
(clutches jacket anxiously, fondles gloves lovingly, glares suspiciously at children who examine his hat, etc.)
How seriously does he take the process? How much interest does
he show?
How does the child handle himself?
(skillfully, clumsily, awkwardly, easily, etc.)
Is his ability equal to the task?
Does he have specific abilities?
(can put on hat but not buckle it, fasten buttons, zipper jacket,
etc.)

It sounds as though each of these questions requires an answer, as
in a questionnaire. On the contrary, the questions are only reminders
of things to be aware of as you are observing. One item may be far
more important than another for a particular child. Some items may
call for lengthy description and others for none. It all depends on
how a child happens to approach his task.

With your two hands alone you are undoubtedly "short-handed"
as you attempt to help a group get dressed for outdoors, and it may
be hard to get anything written down. On the chance that some
occasions do arise when this is possible, a brief description of behavior
that includes some of the above points might read as follows:

. . . . .

As dressing time was announced, Johnny shouted, "Goody!" and beelined to his locker. He plopped his hat on his head, scooped up his coat and ski-pants, and shuffled over to where the teacher was sitting ready to help the children. "Yippee," he gloated. "Here's my pants. Put 'em down for me!" T. laid them out straight and Johnny pretzeled into a sitting position, dropping his coat on the floor. With lightning speed he forced first one foot and then another into the legs of the ski-pants, then wiggled himself into a standing position. Still wiggling his torso, he hauled the straps over his shoulders and reached down for his coat. He looked at it speculatively a moment and then handed it to the teacher. Turning his back to her, he waited for her to hold it in position. As he pulled it up, unmindful of the tucked in collar, he fumbled with the buttons in an obvious effort to make haste.

· · · ·

There are still other reactions to be aware of in routine situations because they extend the implications of the action.

Does the child seem to want to function independently?
How do you know?
How does he behave in relation to the group situation?
Can he proceed in the midst of group activity?
Does he withdraw? Does he get silly or otherwise disruptive?
What are the external factors that may be influencing his reactions?
(This is the dynamic aspect of the *setting* mentioned above.)
Does the teacher sit in one spot and expect the children to come to her?
Are the children expected to sit in their chairs and wait for the teacher's help?
Are the children expected to do the job alone?
How much individual attention is offered?
As much as the child wants?
As much as the teacher thinks he needs?

We include these many details because everything a child does is a response to *something*, whether it be to feelings within himself or to situations and people *outside* himself. To describe only the action, such as "child runs around the room," and not comment on the entire situation leaves us in the dark as to what the action means. Running around the room at rhythms is one thing, at lunch another, at dressing or clean-up still another! A child responds to a total situation, and this includes people, things, the physical environment, the demands to be met, etc. He responds as a total person, with thought, feeling, and physical activity.

WHAT DOES THE CHILD DO IMMEDIATELY AFTER?

When the dressing is over, we note what the child does then and thus complete the sequence of events from the first stimulus to the last concluding act. Sometimes what a child does immediately after the episode we are observing tells us quite a bit about him.

> Does he accept the group procedure that follows, such as sitting on a chair, on the floor, waiting at the door, etc.?
> Does he run out without waiting for the group or the teacher?
> Does he rush to get the first place at the door?
> Does he show the children what he has done?
> Does he cry? Does he sing? Does he chortle to himself?

This may seem a lot of questioning about so simple a procedure as getting dressed to go outdoors. But there are important clues here for us to pick up, as we shall see when we examine the feelings with which a young child invests these selfsame routines.

The Meaning of Routines to Young Children

Do you ever wonder why some children stand patiently to be buttoned and belted but others scream with rage if you make a move to help them? Why some children are utterly confused by the dressing process and others use the occasion for mad dashing around the room? Why some children burst into tears if they cannot find a mitten and others reveal a fine carelessness about everything connected with their clothing?

Of course we know that individual children are different from one another. But *all* children are different from adults generally, especially in this matter of routines.

For adults, routines are a means to an end. We wash for breakfast, we clean to get a place ready for work again, we dress quickly to get to work. But children understand time and schedule only hazily. Nor are these the criteria by which they guide their activities. For young children, routines are either an end in themselves or a deterrent to the important business of living. For example, washing hands does not necessarily have any connection with lunch at all—it might very well be an opportunity to explore and savor the properties of water, and perhaps of soap and paper towels too! It is an occupation in its own right, with its own enticements. Or it is a silly obstacle in the path of food when you're just too hungry! In the same way, clean-up may have nuisance value because it keeps one from having a last chance at the slide; conversely, it may be a cozy way of feeling groupness with peers under the warmth of your teacher's approval. In any case, the sense of responsibility that motivates adults is at its barest beginnings in early childhood and hardly a reliable ally for the teacher.

The pleasure principle is very, very strong in young children, so that "I want to" is as good a reason as any the teacher might think up, and "I don't feel like it" is a really compelling force. To children, routines have a meaning all their own, and it is not an "adult" meaning. In addition, each individual child may add to the meaning a special flavor out of his own experience. Yet with all this, they want to, and will in time, learn to behave as we do.

The Mechanics Come with Attitudes

Children learn how to behave at the table, the sink, or in any other routine from the adults in their lives. For some adults, efficiency *per se* is so important that adult standards are held up as a model with a certain amount of fretfulness and impatience. For others of us it becomes simpler and easier to do the job ourselves than wait for a child to bungle through it. Still others of us love to do things for children because we enjoy being good to them in that way. In some homes there isn't much time for a child, and he must shift for himself. Quite unconsciously, therefore, as children learn the mechanics of the routines, they absorb attitudes too, not only toward the carrying out of the routine, but toward *themselves* as functioning people. Willy-nilly, from the attitudes of the adults during their learning years, children build up conceptions concerning their level of achievement and their potential abilities, without the chance to compare themselves with other children of their own age and experience.

All this a child has under his belt by the time he gets to school, and careful observation of his behavior at routines will reveal a good deal of it. In addition to his handling of the mechanics of living, we may well see something of his feelings about being dependent on adults, or whether being independent of them means anything to him. Perhaps, too, his feeling of trust or suspicion of adults will appear. These general attitudes come through in relation to the specific tasks we call routines. However, the different routines lend themselves to unique mannerisms and behavior reactions intrinsic to the function, and need to be looked at separately for this reason.

Recording Eating Behavior

In observing an eating situation let us bear in mind the intimacy of mother and child in the child's learning to handle foods. In the back of our minds we might tuck away the observation of pediatricians that most eating difficulties stem from anxiety or pressure on the part of the parent. Something of the child's attitudes toward himself is bound to come through as well as his smoothness of functioning. It is certainly an indication of self-confidence and social strength, for example, if a child takes care of his own body needs when he is well enough coordinated to do so.

DETAILS TO OBSERVE

Setting (table setup, other children, teacher, service, etc.)

What is the child's reaction to the eating situation?
Is he accepting, eager, resistant, choosy?
How seriously or casually does he take eating?

How much food does he eat?
(rather little, two helpings, lots of meat, no vegetables, never gets enough, big portions in comparison to others, etc.)

What is his manner of eating?
How does he hold utensils? Does he eat with his hands?
Does he play with food, throw food, hold food in his mouth?
Is he systematic and well organized in his attack on food?
Is he messy, fastidious, etc.?

Does he socialize, and how much?
To whom does he speak? How else does he make contact with children?
Is the socializing more meaningful to him than the eating?
Does he manage both socializing and eating?
Does he talk only to the teacher, to a special friend, to no one, etc.?

Does he show interest in food?
Has he special likes and dislikes?
Does he comment about the food?
What is his pace (speed or slowness) of eating?

What is the adult's role?
>What group procedures are laid down?
>How much and what kind of individual attention are offered?

What is the sequence of events?
>What does the child do and say?
>What does the adult do and say?

How does the child leave the table?
>(talking eagerly, smacking his lips, stonily, in tears, etc.; pushes chair back easily, knocks chair down, etc.)

What does he do then?
>(runs around the room, stands around talking, stands and waits for the teacher, gets himself a book or toy, goes to the toilet, goes to food wagon to help clean plates, looks into bowls for more food, etc.)

HOW SELECTIVE SHALL WE BE?

Since young children are as likely as not to be unconcerned about table manners, we may find ourselves recording activity which is not socially acceptable, with the uneasy thought that putting it down on paper somehow carries our approval. Neither approval nor disapproval plays any part in recording technique, although they may influence what we do or say as we respond to children. To guide children on the long road to maturity we must start with them where they are, which means, first of all, noting accurately what they do without moral bias or judgment. To deny the reality of their behavior because it is displeasing to us or because we are showing them better techniques is to limit ourselves unduly as teachers. It is only human to be subjectively selective about what we observe and record; therefore we must take pains to incorporate a little of the scientific approach into our professional selves. Whatever a child does is part of him and should be recorded.

EATING RECORD

In the following record, eight two- to five-year-olds remained for lunch with two teachers. The children were out in the yard, most of them at the slide.

. . . . .

T. "O.K. Take your last slide and come in and wash your hands for lunch."

Cindy (3¾, pale-skinned, blondish, thin, with delicate, pretty features) took her turn on the slide and then walked quietly indoors. She was one of the first to finish washing; she walked resolutely into the room where the table was set, and sat down. She put her arm around the back of the seat next to her and, when another child tried to sit there, protested mutely and the child took another seat.

T. came in from the bathroom and sat in the seat saved for her by Cindy.

T. "Children, when I ask you, I want you to tell me what you want." She then listed the various kinds of food she had for sandwiches. Cindy quickly and quietly said, "I want tuna fish." She leaned against T. and watched her make a sandwich for another child. Her mouth was open, as if she could not breathe through her nose. When T. gave Cindy her sandwich, she immediately took a bite, chewed slowly and thoroughly with her mouth open, and then took a drink of milk. She continued to eat steadily, putting a little more than the ordinary amount of energy into chewing since she had to keep her mouth open to breathe. As she ate, she looked at the other children, aware of what was going on but not participating in the conversation. When the other T. passed her with a plate of cucumbers, Cindy reached for a piece, nodding her head.

T. asked if the children remembered what she had said she would buy for dessert. Many of the children said, "Watermelon," but Cindy said nothing.

When Cindy finished her sandwich, having used her fingers to help free the food that clung to her teeth, she said to T., "I want peanut butter." While T. made a sandwich for her, Cindy leaned back in her chair, arms behind the back of the chair, kicking her feet, and smiling as she watched T.

T., handing sandwich to Cindy, "Here, Cindy."

Cindy. "Thank you." She immediately began to eat her sandwich. She then drank her milk thirstily, finishing it in several big gulps, and asked T. for more milk.

Boyd. "I squeezed milk in my hand."

Cindy looked at him. T. and children began to talk about milking cows. Cindy listened intently as she continued to eat, but didn't say anything. When a child dropped his cup, she looked under the table for it. As she listened, she jiggled her feet under the table, licked the food off her fingers, and continued to eat. The conversation about cows continued. Cindy interjected, in a quiet voice, "You know what I once—" but another child interrupted her and Cindy didn't finish. She continued to eat, listening to the others. She smiled at Linda who was sitting next to her. Linda accidentally kicked Cindy's feet. Cindy said, "No," whinily, to Linda. T. said, "You put your feet down and she'll put her feet down." And that settled the matter.

Recording Toileting Behavior

As in eating, the toileting routine has its specifically important aspects, such as a child's attitude toward his own body and the important question of whether he sees body functioning and control as a source of pride in achievement or a bond to babyhood.

DETAILS TO OBSERVE

What set the child off? (What is the stimulus?)
(child's own need, imitation of a friend, response to group practice, request by the teacher, wet pants, etc.)

What is his reaction—acceptance or resistance?
(he might obviously need to go to the toilet but refuse to use the school toilet; he might not go when the group goes; he might go cheerfully, absent-mindedly, hurriedly, casually, etc.)

Are there signs of tension? fears?
(stiffness of body, clutching at pants, whimpering, etc.)

How interested does he seem to be?
How seriously or casually does he take the toileting procedure?

How does he handle himself? Are his coordination and skill up to the task?
(Is he competent? awkward? smooth? clumsy? slow? fast?)

What is his manner like?
Casual? Excessively modest? Exhibitionistic? Does he show awareness of sex differences? Does he show interest in sex differences or similarities? What kinds of contacts with children, if any?

Of course, the behavior has to be seen against the background of the group procedures and teacher role to which the child is reacting at the moment. As in other episodes, we record the sequence of events from beginning to end, and if possible, we include the language of the child exactly as we hear it (or note its absence in everything we record). These illustrations may make this clearer.

TOILETING RECORDS

Lorna, age 4½:
Riding on a seesaw with Priscilla. Hops off. "I almost wet my pants." Runs inside, Priscilla following. Both pull down panties and sit on toilets, singing. "Skit, scoot, skit, scoot." Flushes toilet, pulls up underwear and overalls. "I think I'll wash my hands." Removes jacket.

"See I have two shirts, isn't that funny? Are you going to wash your hands too, Priscilla?" Washes quickly. "Now I'll go into the dressing room and see how I look."

．　．　．　．　．

Four-year-old Robert is not so casual:

Robert is in the play yard, standing on top of the packing case, holding his pants and jiggling up and down. Sees teacher and says, "I want to go into the building."

T. "All right. Do you want to go to the toilet?" "Yes." Climbs down hastily, saying, "I don't want you to watch."

T. "I'll close the door. Do you want the seat up?" Robert frowns for a moment. "No, I don't know yet what I'm going to do. I want the door all the way closed."

Teacher closes the door and waits. Robert calls out twice, "I'm not through yet." After several minutes, he shouts, "I'm finished now." Flings open the door and struts out.

T. "Do you want to wash your hands?"

Robert's brows go up in surprise. "No, 'cause then I'd be ready for juice and crackers and it isn't time." Skips out to play yard. Plays in water tub, splashing hands madly. Holds up hands, fingers spread wide. Grins. "Look at my hands—clean!"

．　．　．　．　．

Another view, this time of some Threes:

At the end of the story, the teacher reminded the children to go to the toilet if they had to, before washing up for snack. Martin got up slowly, dreamily, curiously watching the others as they clamored, "I did. I didn't." He says nothing and suddenly walks over to bathroom, by which time three girls were already in it. Lois and Paula are on the seats and Wendy is standing waiting. Martin edges past Wendy into a tight little corner between the sink and the wall. He is completely absorbed in watching Lois, who is now wiping herself. She wiggles off the toilet. "Wendy, I'm finished," she says and begins to pull up her underwear and overalls. Martin comes out of the corner just then and kneels down in front of her. Without saying a word, he holds down her overalls and panties with one hand, and pulls up her shirt with the other. She watches him. He has a look of innocent wonder as he carefully, with one finger, pokes her navel. She is as absorbed as he. They say nothing. The other children are by now watching him. The teacher says to Lois, "You had better move out of there, Lois, because these children are waiting." Martin and Lois both look up at her and Lois pulls up her pants as Martin walks out to wash. He did not go to the toilet.

．　．　．　．　．

Recording Behavior at Resting Time

Rest as a routine has its own particular kind of responses too. Along with such reactions as show trust in adults and acceptance of group patterns, is the matter of body tensions and ability to relax. This is especially significant for the child who is new to the school situation. Even after adjusting to school, however, some children continue to need comfort and support during rest hour, while others have their most successful social experiences then, and still others just drop right off to sound slumber. It may help to see the meaning of resting time to a child in the following terms.

DETAILS TO OBSERVE

How does the child happen to be resting? (What is the stimulus?)
　　Did he sprawl out by himself, or is there a prescribed time?
　　Did the teacher decide he was tired?
　　Does rest automatically follow lunch hour?
　　Does the child seem to understand what is expected of him?
What is his reaction?
　　Accepts (in matter-of-fact fashion, with pleasure, etc.)
　　Resists (dawdles, talks, does not respond, frequently asks to go to the toilet, frequently requests water, etc.)
　　Refuses (cries, runs around the room, runs out of the room, etc.)
Does he require special attention from adult?
　　(patting, sitting nearby, given lollipop, taken to separate room, etc.)
Are there any signs of tension while resting?
　　Body tensions?
　　(amount of movement, restlessness)
　　Comforting devices?
　　(thumb-sucking, masturbation, ear-pulling, etc.)
　　Special attachments?
　　(dolls, animals, handkerchiefs, blankets, pillow, diaper, etc.)
　　Leaving cot frequently on one pretext or another?
What are his bodily requirements for rest?
　　Are there evidences of fatigue?
　　(yawning, red eyes, peevishness, frequent falling, etc.)
　　Does he sleep? For how long?
　　Does he need something to play with?
　　(book, doll, etc.)
　　If he does not sleep, does he seem relaxed?

What is his reaction to group during rest?
  Is it disturbing and disrupting?
    (shouts, sings loudly, runs about, crawls under children's cots, pulls up blinds, annoys children, etc.)
  Is there social activity?
    (talks to neighbor, signals, etc.)
  Is he conscious of other children's needs?
    (whispers, walks quietly, etc.)
  How does he wake?
    (smiling, talking, whimpering, crying, tired, refreshed, etc.)
  What does he do when he wakes?
    (lies quietly, calls the teacher, rushes to the bathroom, starts to play, etc.)

· · · · ·

Teacher is seated near a group of five four-year-olds who are lying quietly on their cots. Jeff is having a little difficulty getting comfortable. He tosses restlessly about, occasionally playing with his hands and feet. Near his head is a Teddy Bear which he tosses up into the air from time to time and tries to catch, unsuccessfully, with one hand. With a jerk and a grumble he is under his blanket and out again. He stretches onto his side, with finger in his mouth and looking tired. All of a sudden he is hidden again under the blanket, whispering barely audibly to himself. At times one of the other teachers walks through the room to the coat closet. Jeff raises his head long enough to watch her get her purse and leave. Then he drops back onto the cot, repeating his starting performance—playing with his hands and feet, as well as the fringe on the edge of his blanket. He stares dreamily at the chairs and beds around the room, all the while playing with his hands, feet, or blanket fringe. Suddenly he starts to clap loudly. Teacher cautions him about this, explaining that this is rest hour and children are sleeping. He stares at the teacher for a moment and then lies back without as much as a sound until the end of rest hour.

· · · · ·

Patterns of Behavior

Observations of children's behavior during the daily routines at school reveal behavior at any given moment in a child's life. Many such on-the-spot observations, added up over a period of time, reveal that which is consistent and repetitive in a child's responses to similar situations. We can then see his particular patterns of response, which may be similar to or different from other children's but, in any case, are true of him. A pattern of behavior may be fixed and steady, even to rigidity, or it may be shifting and changing, even to the point of utter unpredictability. Over a really long period of time (six months to a year) the records may reveal sharply changing patterns as the child learns to handle routines differently, with maturing and experience. The importance of the on-the-spot record taken over time is the evidence that is accumulated to support or dispute the generalizations we usually feel able to make after we have known a child for a while. This is a basic reason for attempting frequent recording, even though admittedly it does not come easily in the life of a teacher.

This is one child's *pattern of behavior* at rest hour:

Tony's face always puckered up when he saw the shades drawn, although the look of distress never developed as far as tears. Not until the teacher came to sit with him did he relax, and then noticeably. He never asked for anything to comfort him, like a toy or a lollipop, and never said anything. But as the teacher sat quietly near his cot, he would fall asleep in five minutes.

. . . . .

A *changing pattern* is revealed in this end-of-the-year generalization about a child's behavior at dressing time:

At the beginning of the year Nancy would rush to get to the door the minute her outdoor clothes were on. She would lean against it stiffly with arms and legs outstretched and look like a formidable opponent for anyone who might challenge her. Many times she fought verbally with Peter and John, the only ones in the group who dared question her right to be "first" all the time. As her friendship with Susan and Kate grew, she began to urge them to hurry and be first with her. Since Susan and Kate enjoy conversation too much to be hurried, she got nowhere with this. She would look anxiously at the door as she prodded them and eventually run off to her coveted spot. But one day Nancy stayed and waited for Susan and Kate. Triumphantly she confided to them, "We don't care if we're not first, do we, huh?" This was a great day for Nancy!

. . . . .

The patterns do not always rise to meet us. We may have to hunt for them deliberately. It helps to go back, say after two or three months, and tease out the items pertaining to that aspect of behavior we are trying to check. We might do something like this:

Episodes of resting −9/13, 9/21, 11/9, 1/8, 3/14
Episodes of toileting−9/14, 9/27, 10/17, 12/7, 3/14
Episodes of dressing−9/17, 10/3, 1/22

Episodes of eating —9/24, 10/12, 1/8, 4/13
etc., etc.

Listing the highlights of the individual episodes helps make the pattern become clear.

Highlights of Tommy's resting behavior:

9/23   Tommy cried when he woke from rest.
9/30   Tommy clung to teacher as he woke.
10/6   Tommy would not fall asleep without teacher sitting next to him.

The consistency of behavior is rather obvious. Tommy's rest time at school is fraught with feelings of uncertainty at this point.

Generalizing from the Records

A child is all of one piece, but different situations may cause him to react in different ways. In finding his pattern of reaction to different routines, we might find similarity in all—or positive or negative reactions to different ones. For example, he might be cheerfully cooperative in all school routines, or silently withdrawn; or he might be a fine group member until toileting, or eating, or rest. His reactions in any case are uniquely his, and the record tells us about his unique responses to the life situations at school. In gathering evidence bit by bit and then seeing the patterns emerge, we really begin to see the child as he actually is. These persistent or changing patterns of behavior can be grouped under broad generalizations. The following are useful in understanding a child's behavior during the routines.

PERSISTENT OR CHANGING PATTERNS OF BEHAVIOR
IN RELATION TO ROUTINES: A SUMMARY

Usual attitudes at beginning, throughout, and at end of routine
Accepts easily, complies, resists directly or indirectly, shows signs of tensions, fears
Degree of interest

Dependence or independence as evidenced in routines
Has to be reminded or told
Acts on his own responsibility and initiative
Accepts or rejects assistance

Consistent emotional reactions to routines
(excitement, silliness, relaxation, self-confidence, etc.)

Coordination and abilities, tempo and time length

Effect of child's behavior on group functioning

Routines as social experience

Adult participation and child response
To group procedures established by adults
To individual attention

Expression of physical functioning
Amount of food eaten, length of sleep, frequency of urination, ability to relax, need for rest

Awareness of and interest in own sex and sex differences revealed through routines

Special problems (excesses)
Excessive modesty or exhibitionism at toileting, dressing and undressing
Attachment to clothes
Extreme choosiness at eating time, retaining food, not eating, inability to eat solid foods, etc.
Dreaminess
Excessive physical tension and inability to relax
Fetishes
Excessive need for attention from teacher
Special ways in which teacher handles this child, and why
Wetting, soiling (in relation to age and frequency)

RECORDS SHOWING TEACHERS' GENERALIZATIONS

The following are illustrations of records in which the teacher has generalized about the child's behavior at routines on the basis of many on-the-spot records and the patterns that emerged.

Upon entering school, Lee resisted vigorously any and all routines, gradually accepting them one by one. He has never had a toilet accident at school, but called for the utmost privacy in toileting and usually postponed the process until he reached home. It was not until December that he went willingly without signs of stress. I was delighted last week to have him come to me and say, "You know, I went to the bathroom twice already." He knows when we wash hands and washes his in methodical fashion. He eats his snack matter-of-factly, placing cup and napkin in wastebasket when finished. He rests quietly after settling down on his rug. He dresses and undresses himself, asking for help only when necessary. He knows where to hang his clothes, and is careful to hang them up correctly.

. . . . .

Kay is fully independent now in dressing and undressing and no longer asks for help. Toileting is handled entirely by herself and even our presence is not required. Resting is still a time for socializing but for the most part without too much giggling. If she has been playing hard, she usually stops periodically to sit and look at a book or just watch what is going on around her as she sits. This rest period sometimes lasts for ten minutes, then off she goes again.

· · · · ·

In routines as in other activities Nora at first did everything for herself and did it well. Could dress and undress herself with a minimum of help, even to buttoning. When given stool to stand on, she could turn on faucets after she had been shown how. In few records available on toileting, I have noticed no great curiosity as to differences of sex, with the exception of mentioning that she sits down to make and Craig stands up. She does not even look too much, but shows great interest in how fast the water or urine runs down the toilet and "how down it goes." Toileting time for Nora is noted to be a time for socializing. In the beginning she didn't want anyone to wash with her, but at present will wash in bowl with two others. Teacher on duty says Nora at this time very often talks about happenings of the morning past and most often has a remark about the following juice and rest routines. These remarks themselves have a repetitive quality. "Juice is good." "I sleep on my rug." "Show you my rug." As to juice routine, Nora in the beginning watched the children to see how they acted, what they had, what they did with their cups, etc. If someone singled her out for attention, she acted coy or grimaced or performed for the child, but hesitated when she noticed adults looking. Now for the most part she eats quickly and wants to hurry up to rest. Nora passes the basket with cookies in it to each child in order around the table, then on to the next table, until all three tables have been served. In comparison with many of the four-year-olds' procedure, this is much more systematic. She has never rested quietly on her mat, but at first she flopped up and down on her tummy, pulling on others' rugs when they did this to hers. Now she has a very hard time to lie on the mat at all, but wants to stand and grimace and dance before the floor-length mirror. When reminded to get on her mat, she drops down quickly, rests rigidly for a few seconds, and very often never does more than just sit. In all routines Nora appears to enjoy socializing. She seems to feel comfortable in following routines, even most of the rest periods. During rest, if Nora's rug is where she is less likely to disturb the group, we do not enforce rest on her as long as she is just moving and not talking. She does not seem to be tired or need rest.

· · · · ·

The generalizations based on what we see happening tell us something about matters that are of vital importance to young children. Adults who developed social acceptability in these areas long ago, and perform correctly with ease and without thought, are likely to overlook their significance in children's growing concepts of themselves as people in a social environment.

4

RECORDING A CHILD'S USE OF MATERIALS

The Meaning of Materials to Children

WE turn now to another area of functioning in the life of a child, his experiences with materials. Play materials are as integral a part of school life as routines, but their function in the development of personality is somewhat different. If we tend to see play materials as a means of keeping idle hands busy, or if we evaluate their use in terms of work, we are likely to miss the special role they do play.

Materials, ordinary play materials, are a bridge between the child's inner self and the outside world. They are the means by which a child captures impressions of the world outside himself and translates them into forms he can understand; they are the means of pulling out of himself what he feels and giving it concrete expression. His inexperience limits his grasp of the world he lives in, and his speech is not yet the most efficient tool for the expression of ideas and feelings about this world. Materials (toys, blocks, sand, paint, clay, wood, paper, crayons, pencils, etc.) help him to . . .

. . . transform feelings into action.
> Anger or high spirits get pounded into clay.
> The desire to be big and strong goes into building "the tallest building in the world."
> The mood of spring sunshine is gently painted in pinks, yellows, and pale greens.

. . . translate ideas into forms, concepts into shapes.
> A house of blocks, like a real house, has to be closed in and around; a road of blocks rambles on and on; a bridge is high up and across.

. . . turn impressions into products.
> A cookie of clay must be round and flat; a crayoned grown-up has long legs and a big smile.

26

Even if his impressions of a tree, a cow, and his daddy all come out looking like a blob of red paint, a child feels he has made a good try! Through his use of materials, a child externalizes impressions and feelings, develops muscles and skills, grows in his powers of reasoning and logic. He gains in inner strength as he clarifies his hazy, incomplete understanding of the real world of objects, phenomena, and people.

A child approaches materials as he approaches life itself, with directness or shyness, with attack or withdrawal, with fear and hesitancy or with courage and self-confidence. Do all children plunge into soapsuds with the same zest? Do all children build daring block towers? Do all children sprawl paints across every inch of paper? Don't we all know the tidy child who handles clay and paint almost daintily? Or the cheerful little fellow who is never willing to stop playing and put toys away, makes the most mess at the clay table, carries the mess over into an orgy of soap and water in the bathroom, and disappears just when he's needed to clean up! And what of the many others who confine themselves to a limited few of the materials we offer them, as though starving themselves in the midst of plenty? Or the sad child who does not play with anything? There is a consistency of style and approach to materials that reveals much about children's responses.

Children will take any material, shape, or form and breathe a bit of themselves into it. The more shapable, or "unstructured," the material is, the better it serves for them to project feelings and ideas. At first contact, a material is something outside oneself, and a curiosity for that reason. It has to be explored as an item of the world outside of self. Then there is experimentation with it for its own sake: What are its properties and possibilities? Does it stick, stretch, break, fall, crush, smear? Eventually the material becomes a medium for expression and projection, and it is *used* for the child's own purposes. When a child is fairly well able to break down the details that pertain to objects and people, and he has the physical coordination for detailed work, he may use materials representationally to crystallize that clarity. If he is confused about some details, the confusion is set down too. Interestingly enough, if his feelings are stronger than his intellectual curiosity or creativity, he may seem to misuse the material, as when he makes mud out of clay or uses a doll for poking and throwing, or deliberately breaks block buildings. At such a point, he may need materials that are especially suited to his needs.

Materials that have a specific use and function, like dolls and bikes, are "structured" materials. Children use these for the implied purpose, but they will also project feelings onto them. (The doll is naughty and rebellious or is crying and upset.) Or children use them as a means for carrying out ideas, desires, or fantasies. (The bike is a plane, the doll is a big girl, the lotto cards are tickets, etc.)

Semi-structured materials, like blocks (not as fluid as paint or clay, nor as finally formed as a toy car), give the satisfaction of construction and three-dimensional solidity.

But beyond this analysis, there remains the wonder of children's imagination: If they need a plane, a car or a stick can become one, and if they want to make a person, they will struggle with the material until the essence of *person* is there.

In short, materials are used by children in the way children themselves need and want to use them. The manner and style, however, is unique to each child.

Details to Observe in Recording a Child's Use of Materials

THE SETTING
Include the nearby significant people and activities, as in routines, and also such things as the abundance or scarcity of materials, availability of supplies, amount and kind of adult supervision, etc.

THE STIMULUS
How does the child come to use the material?
(teacher-suggested; group procedure; imitation of another child; self-initiated; suggested by another child, etc.)

RESPONSE TO *Paint*
What colors does the child use? Does he mix colors (in jars or on the paper)? Are the colors separated on paper?
Does he paint one color over another?
Is he able to control the drips?
Does he try to control the drips? Does he deliberately drip?
Does he confine himself to one small spot or bit of space, or does he spread out? Does he paint off the paper?
What forms, if any?
(vertical lines, curves, circles, fill-ins, letters, dots, numbers, blotches of color, representation, etc.)
Does he paint over the forms?

What kind of brush strokes?
  (scrubbing, dotting, gliding, etc.)
How many paintings? Does he paint quickly? Does he work for a
  long time on one?
Does he name the painting? In detail? In general?

RESPONSE TO *Clay*
How does he handle the clay physically?
  (pounding, rolling, pulling apart; squeezing, poking, making
  mush, making balls, snakes; slapping it, stamping on it; patting,
  stroking, scraping, etc.)
Does he use supplementary tools, such as tongue depressors?
  (sticks, toothpicks, scissors, beads, etc.)
Is there representation?
  (naming; size of products; accuracy of detail)
How does he use material in the space available? Does he work in
  his own area or does he spread out?
  (off the board, over the table, etc.)

RESPONSE TO *Blocks*
What blocks does the child select?
  (size and type of blocks; supplementary materials—dolls, small
  blocks, cars, wedgies, etc.)
What forms does he construct?
  (up in the air, crisscross, along the floor, piling, enclosures, recog-
  nizable structures, etc.)
How does he use space?
  (confined, spread out; close to shelves; aware of obstacles; etc.)
Is the structure named? Is it used in dramatic play? Is the child
  interested primarily in the process of building?

LENGTH OF TIME SPENT WITH MATERIAL

Records of Use of Materials

  Two-year-old Penny at the sandbox:
Penny runs to sandbox carrying tablespoon, empty orange juice can,
and toy plastic teacup. She climbs down into sandbox, sits down in
corner, and silently and intently begins to fill can with sand, using
spoon. She is oblivious to several other children around her. She stands
up, dumps sand from can onto asphalt outside sandbox. She bangs
can down on sand several times, then gently pats sand with open
palm, saying "Cake." Rene, aged four, comes up. She starts to take
can from Penny, saying, "Can I have that?" Penny pulls the can
away and stands still, staring at Rene. Teacher gives Rene a small
spoon and plastic cup. She stands beside Penny and they both begin
to spoon sand, occasionally smiling at each other. Penny climbs out

of the sand to bench where teacher is sitting. She dumps the sand onto the bench and then spoons it back into can. She dumps it onto the bench again, and pats it gently. "I'm making cake." She takes a spoonful of sand and puts it on teacher's hand. She looks up and sees Patty on the swing. She runs over to her, carrying spoon with her . . .

．　．　．　．　．

Four-year-old Leo at the paints:

Leo wanders into the art room, pausing at the door to watch Polly, who is painting at the easel, and Mary and Ellen who are drawing with chalk.

"Guess I'll paint, O.K.?"

Without awaiting an answer, Leo carefully lifts smock from hook, carries it, bundled in his arms, to teacher. "Mrs. S., put this on for me?" Teacher helps him into smock and he bounces over to easel next to Polly. Looks into jars on her easel, looks at colors in his own jars.

"I have red. And yellow too."

Picks up a brush in each hand, hands rotate in opposite directions. Stops, still holding brushes aloft. Looks at paper and smiles. "That's the way spiders are made. Spiders are nice. When I was a snake I was friendly with them and I liked it."

Dips brushes into paint and resumes swirling motions, dripping paint with gay abandon.

"I don't like to wipe on the edge of jars. I just do it this way. Don't you think I'm covering this whole paper up? I am."

Dips brushes again. "There's hard painting at the bottom, Teacher." (sediment) Inspects tips of brushes and paints drip off onto floor. Looks at teacher, frowning and worried-looking. "It's all right if paint gets on the paper, isn't it?" Waits, brushes held over tray, for reply. When reassured, he makes a few tentative jabs at the paper with the brushes.

"That's all for me." Replaces brushes carefully in correct colors, unbuttons smock slowly, and strips it off, dropping it to floor.

"I'll save my brushes till tomorrow, right?" Strolls out to sink, rolling up sleeves as he goes.

．　．　．　．　．

The Unique Quality of the Child, or HOW he does WHAT

Thus far we have recorded a child's use of materials in such a way as to get a fairly inclusive picture of *what* he is doing. But we do not see from this picture what the special meaning of the experience is to him. We are not getting down *how* he does the thing he is doing.

To show a child's feelings as he uses materials, we must consciously and deliberately include, along with the actual action itself, the signs that show feeling. When we record *gross* movement, such as "he reached for a block," "he lifts the brush," "he grabbed the sponge," we are recording actions completely objectively, but without their life-pulse, or even our own response to their meaning. A child might be reaching for that block stealthily, hesitantly, or victoriously; perhaps he grabbed the sponge angrily, defiantly, efficiently, or just quickly; and he could lift the brush suspiciously, hastily, or absentmindedly. It is not enough to record what he does (i.e., he reached for a block); we must tell HOW he does the WHAT. In the above descriptions, the meaning of each activity is different with each qualifying word. The descriptive adjective or adverb sums up the details we have been recording, and indicates the unique character of the gross action.

As we live and work with people, we react spontaneously to their range of feelings without ever thinking about how we know they feel as they do. We just sense it. With children, we certainly sense when they are delighted with themselves, when they are unhappy, when they are tense, when they are completely at ease. Actually, we take into our mind's eye a wide variety of cues that the other person sends out and get a composite picture which we then interpret according to our own experience and associations. Often we jump to conclusions before we get all the clues. It helps, therefore, to break down the nuances of behavior so that we are able to include them in the record. Even though something of our own interpretation will be there, the evidence to support us will be there too.

These clues to feeling that we must record are the involuntary, non-controlled, non-directed movements and gestures that accompany any gross action and give it its character. They are unique for every child and every action, for no child works at materials, or any form of play, without a variety of accompanying behavior. Thus, as we pick up his motions . . .

. . . we include the sounds that he makes and the language he speaks.
    If he is using his voice, what is it like?
        (jubilant, wavering, ringing, well-modulated, whining, etc.)
    To whom is it directed?
        (himself, other children, teacher, no one in particular, etc.)
    What does he say? (direct quote)
        (chants, sings; nonsense syllables, phrases, stories, etc.)

. . . we note the movements of his body as he uses materials.
> What is his posture like?
>> (erect, rigid, hunched, floppy, straight, curled, squat, etc.)
> What is the rhythm of his body movement?
>> (jerky, smooth, easy, jumpy, staccato-like, flowing, etc.)
> What is the tempo of his body movement?
>> (rapid, sluggish, measured, slow, swift, leisurely, deliberate, speedy, hasty, moderate, unhurried, etc.)
> How much and what kind of effort does he expend?
>> (a great deal, excessive, very little, moderate; strained, laborious, easy, vigorous, forceful, feeble, etc.)
> What kind of freedom does he show in his body movement?
>> (sweeping movements; cramped, tiny movements; free-flowing; restrained, tight, restricted, etc.)

. . . we identify the details of facial expression.
> Eyes—(glint, dullness, brightness, shine, teariness, blinking, etc.)
> Mouth—(grin, quiver, pucker, tongue between lips, biting lips, smiling, wide open, drawn tight, etc.)

From these details we can surmise the child's emotional response to the materials, e.g., excitement, contentment, frustration, self-critical-ness, confidence, squeamishness, stimulation, overstimulation, taking in stride, intense interest, preoccupation, etc.

Reactions to People Around Him

The .feelings which the child reveals may be reactions to things other than the materials he is using. We include in the record, there-fore, what we see of his reactions to the people around him:

> Is there any socializing with children as the child uses materials?
>> How does the child show awareness of children about him?
>>> (talking, showing materials and products, touching others, etc.; using products in dramatic play; helping others, criticizing; calling for attention to what he is doing, etc.)
>> Does he work alone or with others?
> What are his relations to adults while using materials?
>> (calls for help, approval, supplies, etc.)
>> (is suggestible, defiant, indifferent, heedless, mindful, etc., re-garding adult offers of help, adult participation, reminders of rules and limitations, offers of suggestions, etc.)
> How does the experience end?
>> What events and feelings follow immediately after?
>>> (puts things away, puts his work on the storage shelf, destroys

his work, shows things to the children or teachers, leaves everything and goes to another activity, dances around the room,
etc.)

Records Illustrating Detail

The following records show increasing attention to detail. The
first is primarily a recording of gross movements and sequence of
events.

Marsha, age 5:
Marsha came directly to the outdoor table on which teachers had
prepared a basket of scissors, crayons, paste in a six-ounce jar with a
spoon in it, and small 1½-inch cups. The children were encouraged to
help themselves to the paste and to put it in a cup. There was also a
stack of paper and two aluminum plates filled with paper collage,
string and wool, and cloth collage in various shapes.

"I wanna paste, I wanna paste, I wanna paste."
Teacher, busy with another child, "Yes, Marsha. It's Debby's turn
now. . . . It will be yours next. Help yourself, Marsha."
(Marsha can be very self-sufficient, but now and again becomes
completely helpless, usually with a smile on her face as though she
knows she is acting.)
Standing in the same place, and not looking at teacher, Marsha
says, in a babyish, whiny tone, "I wanna paste, I wanna paste." She
looks along the table at the others who are cutting, crayoning, pasting.
She moves around a child, and helps herself to the entire basket of
crayons, placing it in front of her seat. She helps herself to paper,
sits down, and makes a few crayon marks. As though realizing that
this was not what she had planned to do, she calls, "Mrs. M.?"
"Yes?"
"I wanna paste."
"The jar is down at the end of the table, Marsha."
Marsha goes for the paste and gives herself some. Back at her
seat she pastes a piece of collage on her paper, helps herself to another
piece, and pastes that. She works intently, lips parted. Spends more
time than needed pushing her finger around and around in the paste
on the paper, as though enjoying the feel of it. She pastes wool, lace,
paper, and cloth. A piece of string frustrates her. T. approaches.
"May I help you?"
"Yes," whiny and a little pouty. T. puts a short line of paste on
the paper and lays the string on it.
"Now you show me how you want your string to go and we will
put some paste there," Marsha accepts this idea.
"Now you put the paste where you want the string to be." She
does.

"I'm finished!"

"O.K."

She smears, smears the paste around on her hands.

"I wanna wash."

"There's water and towels on the tree stump," says the teacher.

Marsha washes and runs off to the trikes. She had not spoken to any child while she worked.

. . . . .

The second record has more of the "qualifying" details, and reveals the mood of the child more successfully.

Winky, age 4¾, at the paints:

Winky points to the window and with radiant face calls in delight, "It's snowing cherry blossoms! First they are white, then green, then red, red, red! I want to paint!" He goes to the easel and quickly snatches up a smock. Sliding in beside Wayne, he whispers to him caressingly and persuasively, "Wayne, you want blue? I give it to you, okay? You give me red because I'm going to make cherries, lots of red cherries!"

After the boys exchanged paint jars, Winky sits erect, and with a sigh of contentment starts quickly but with clean strokes to ease his brush against the edge of the jar. He makes dots all around the outer part of the paper. His tongue licks his upper lip, his eyes shine, his body is quiet but intense. The red dots are big, well-rounded, full of color, and clearly separated. While working, Winky sings to himself, "Red cherries, big, round red cherries!" The first picture completed, he calls the teacher to hang it up to dry. The next picture starts as the first did, dots at the outside edge, but soon filling the whole paper. He uses green too, but the colors do not overlap.

Still singing his little phrase, Winky paints a third and fourth picture, concentrating intently on his work.

The other children pick up his song and Wayne starts to paint blue dots on his paper. Waving his brush, Winky asks, "Wayne, want to try my cherries?" Swiftly and jubilantly he swishes his brush across Wayne's chin. Laughing, he paints dots on his own hands. "My hands are full of cherries," he shouts. He runs into the adjoining room, calling excitedly to the children, "My hands are full of cherries!" He strides into the bathroom emphatically to wash his hands. Susie follows him in, calling, "Let's see, Winky." "Ha, I ate them all," he gloats as he shows his washed hands with a sweeping movement. He grabs a toy bottle from the shelf, fills it with water and asks the teacher to put the nipple on. He lies down then on a mattress and contentedly sucks the bottle, his face softly smiling, his eyes big and gazing into space, his whole body limp with satisfaction.

. . . . .

This record gives us some of the teacher's assessment of the child she is observing.

Freddy, age 5, at clay:

After hanging up his snowsuit Freddy entered the playroom in a manner which for him was thoughtful and quiet, a great contrast to his voluble propulsion, as if shot out of a cannon. He edged into a chair at the end of a table where no one else sat, his eyes dreamily watching in an unfocused manner the actions of others at two other tables as they rolled, punched, and pounded the clay they were using. Like a sleepwalker he accepted a hunk of clay and in an absent manner rolled it under the palm of his right hand, his head turned to the side, eyes directed toward the ten or twelve in the room.

A few minutes passed thus. Then he picked up the hunk of clay and let it fall "kerplunk" on the table. Instantly his mood changed, like pressing a button and changing a still picture into an animated one. "Boom!" he shouted, "I got a ball! Look at my ball, teacher! Bounce! Bounce!" He banged it down a few times. Then he started rolling it into a long thin piece. "Here's a snake. I'm making a rattle-snake. Are you making a rattlesnake, Donna?" he asked the child nearest him at the other table.

To David, who had a moment before entered the room and started to work at Freddy's table, "That's a snowman, David. Now I'm making a snowman. . . . Now I'm making a snake big as Edward's." Freddy held it up and chortled with glee. "Hee-hee-hee. . . ."

"Look what I made. I twist it here." He dropped it on the table and began pounding it.

"Now I'm making a pancake. Look at my pancake. Taste my pancake, teacher."

Flop! he dropped it on the table again, rolling it over and over, faster —faster, his motions in keeping with his words. Head and shoulders were hunched over the table, his lips and tongue stumbled over each other in an effort to increase the speed of his words. "Chee—ee—ee— eeeeeeeee. . . ."

Everything slowed down. He was quiet, absorbedly working for a moment. Then in sharp staccato and prideful tone: "Look what I made, teacher."

"Look what I made, Donna."

"Look at my wrist watch."

At this point it was necessary for the teacher to help another child, and she was in a stooping position, with her back to Freddy. He poked her insistently in the back to add emphasis to his exhortation.

"Look at me, teacher!"

She turned to find the clay covering Freddy's upper lip. His head was tilted back to prevent its slipping off. "It's a mustache. Ha-ha-ha (he laughed uproariously). Now it's a hat." He quickly transferred the clay to his head.

"Teacher, look at my hat."

It seems that Freddy's satisfaction in all he does comes not only from his creative use of materials but from the response of individuals, especially adults, present.

. . . . .

Interpretation—the Last Dimension

Even though we spot the separate, small parts of an action, we actually respond to the whole, integrated behavior of a child, such as his anger, joy, surprise. Our response follows a spontaneous, unspoken assessment of the child's feeling which is drawn from our personal experience and understanding. To some extent we must rely on this subjectivity to define or interpret a child's behavior. We are dependent, however, on correct descriptive words about significant details to place that feeling on record. The value of a record that includes details such as those suggested in the preceding sections is that our interpretation (he is happy, he is sad) is rather better bolstered by objective evidence. We are therefore less likely to be assuming that a feeling is present in a child because we happen to be identifying with him as the underdog or victim, or because we are reacting with subjective antagonism to an aggressor or uncouth person, or because for any other reason we are putting ourselves into the situation irrationally. Interpretation represents the sum total of our background of understanding. Professionally valuable interpretation relies heavily on objective data.

A Note of Caution

It is impossible to get everything into every record. No child ever does everything possible in human behavior, nor could a teacher get it all down if he did. Don't try to use these suggestions as a checklist! While busily checking off what seems important to look for, the child may be doing something we never thought of at all, and you would miss it. Keep your eyes on the youngster. not on the printed page! It is not *how much* you record, but *what* and *how*, that makes a record valuable.

On-the-Spot Records Lead to Supported Generalizations

The review of a child's use of materials over a period of time will be a mirror of his growth in this area. We will get to know many things about him that we might have missed without these concentrated observations of his activity. We will see a profile of his tastes and his ideas and learn how much confidence he has in his own imagination and capacity. We will note his dependency on adults and children for standards and security, his concern with standards or his indifference to them, his pleasure in doing or his anxiety about doing things wrong. These responses are evaluated best when seen against the backdrop of a child's general coordination, maturity, experience, and age, as well as against the usual behavior of children in his age group.

Persistent or Changing Patterns of Behavior
in Relation to Materials: A Summary

As with the summary on routines, we look for patterns of behavior—over-all patterns that indicate a general approach to materials and specific patterns relating to different materials. Here are suggestions for what to include in such a summary:

1. How the child uses the various materials—paint, clay, blocks, etc.—over a period of time, in persistent or changing ways
    How he comes to use the material generally
        (on his own initiative, on the suggestion of the teacher or another child, through imitation of other children)
    Coordination (his physical ability to carry out techniques)
    Techniques (include the stage of development—manipulative, exploratory, representational—in relation to child's age and background of experience. For example, painting dots, rolling clay or piling cubes are techniques which can be early steps in the use of new materials, typical techniques of an age group, or excessively simple usage of material by a child who has the age and background for more complex approaches)
    How he works (concentration and care used; exploratory; competently, skillfully, intensively, carelessly, tentatively, distractible, in different ways)
    Language or sound accompaniments
    Mannerisms

Products (creativity, imagination, originality shown)

Attention span (in general, and in relation to specific materials and activities)

Use of materials in dramatic play—which materials are so used?

Does he complete what he starts?

Adult role and child's response (Indicate rules, limitations, participation, what is permitted, and how child accepts all these.)

2. How the child seems to feel about the materials

Number, variety, frequency of materials and activities enjoyed, used, avoided. (Include changing and static interest.)

General attitudes—enthusiastic, eager, confident, matter-of-fact, cautious, etc. (Include attitude toward new as well as familiar materials.)

Importance of given areas to the child—interest, intensity of pleasure, preoccupation, fears, avoidance, resistance.

In relation to which materials the child apparently feels satisfaction, frustration, self-confidence, inadequacy, etc.

How he reacts to failure, to success (What constitutes failure or success? What is the level of aspiration?)

3. How the child's use of color and form compares with what most children in the group seem to be doing

4. Child-adult relationship revealed via materials
   Independence—dependence

5. Special problems

Distress over breakage, avoidance of messiness, concentration on only one material or idea, inability to concentrate and enjoy

Following are examples of two children's over-all use of materials. The various items from the records, when brought together in a summary of persistent or changing patterns, are easily written up as a sketch of a youngster's use of materials. In time this sketch becomes part of the end-of-the-year record of the child.

RECORDS OF OVER-ALL RESPONSE TO MATERIALS

Lee, age 4 yrs. 5 mos.:

Lee's work with creative materials has been largely teacher-initiated. Before he begins any activity he usually spends more time watching the other children. Then, when he apparently feels sure of himself, he begins. His attention span is adequate to complete the activity. He works deliberately and quietly, absorbed and interested in the task at hand. It is quite evident that this is real work. His work is neat and carefully done. When he abandons this approach to materials he seems worried, and seeks reassurance from the teacher that this untidiness is accepted comfortably by her. He verbalizes as he works, a running commentary to teacher, children, or no one. He shows pride in accomplishment and again often seeks approval from the teacher. His work with clay is delightful and imaginative and he seems to feel more freedom here than in the use of other media.

. . . . .

Iris, age 3:

Materials most used by Iris are sand, mud, crayons, easel paints, finger paints, and water. Just recently she has begun to use the clay to make cakes with cooky cutters or make imprints with any article handy. At first her attitude toward materials was one of indifference, but now she is interested in what she is making and comes to show it to the teachers or children. Paste on her hands at first annoyed her so that she did not want to use it. Today she was pasting and I was delighted to see a paste smear in her hair, and Iris concentrating intently on her creation.

When a new material was introduced she looked at it but did not attempt to play with it. Recently we received train and track, musical bells, new dishes, and started a new project of covering our rug chest. She wanted to be part of each group, except dishes, and went from one thing to another as fast as she could. This was so unusual that we almost gasped in surprise. The part that gave us the biggest thrill was this morning when two children were taken upstairs to cover the chest. Iris went to the toilet and on the way back noticed what was going on. Going up to a big five-year-old she said, "Give me hammer" in a demanding voice. Teacher said she could have a turn next. Stamping foot, trying to pull hammer from Lucy's hand, she replied, "Now, I want it right now." Not receiving it instantly, she came down to tell the other teacher her trouble. She did get a turn and then went to the musical bells. While there are still materials she has not touched, such as blocks, setting table with dishes, cars, she is adding to her play more materials each day. Outside equipment is now, and has been from the beginning, used without fear of falling. Every piece of equipment has been used by her, and with good control of muscles, expression and movement of body indicating extreme satisfaction. The swing is the one place where she always hums and sings.

5

LANGUAGE AS A TOOL IN RECORDING

IT IS obvious that the language of recording presents its own difficulties, especially for people unaccustomed to writing. It is easy to feel the challenge too great and to give the whole thing up as a bad job. Since the important nuances of behavior cannot be recorded adequately without some use of descriptive terminology, we are going to digress here and explore this aspect of the recording technique. It is not at all impossible to grow in skill if you consider that almost everyone has a larger passive vocabulary than an active one. Suppose we joggle our memories for verbs, adverbs, adjectives, and phrases that can be used descriptively.

Verbs

Some of us could think of a dozen synonyms for the word *walk* in a matter of seconds—

amble, stroll, saunter, clomp, stomp, march, strut, ramble, etc.

Others of us get paralyzed at the challenge. Yet the distinction between one child's actions, or gross movements, and another's may depend on the correct synonym for the word *walk*. Look at it this way:

A turkey walks. A cat walks. Are they the same? A one-year-old walks and an octogenarian walks. Their movements are obviously dissimilar. Johnny walks and Susie walks, and we must record the quality of each. To find the exactly characterizing word, we might say the turkey *struts*, the cat *slinks*, the baby *waddles,* the old man *totters,* Johnny *lopes*, and Susie *minces*. The word walk tells us *what a person does* but not *how he does it*. No two children walk across a playroom or over to a child or toward the teacher in exactly the same way. As

40

teachers, we respond to the *quality* of the behavior as we watch the child. We respond to the child who walks frantically because he is in trouble, and we feel in our own muscles the swinging walk of a child who is full of joy.

Here are some synonyms as a starter for verbs commonly used in records. There are many more with which to become familiar.

Run—stampede, whirl, dash, dart, gallop, speed, shoot across, bolt, fly, hippety-hop, dash.

Say—whisper, bellow, shout, scream, roar, lisp, whine, demand, tell, murmur.

Cry—wail, howl, whimper, fuss, bawl, sob, mourn, lament, weep.

Adverbs

Adverbs are one means by which pedestrian verbs can be given character when the exact verb is elusive. They are somewhat interpretative in that we decide the mood and feeling of the behavior when we use them. But as we indicated before, a teacher cannot be absolutely objective, since she herself is a part of the total situation in which the recording occurs. All we ask is that such interpretation be backed up by enough evidence to be reasonably sound. Thus, going back to the verb *walk*, we can say walked merrily, jauntily, briskly, slowly, downheartedly, jubilantly, heavily, etc. Or the ordinary verb *talk* can be narrowed down meaningfully when excitedly, pleasantly, sourly, resentfully, cheerfully, cheerily, laughingly, etc., are tacked on.

Adjectives

We need a good supply of adjectives too. For example, is every smile a cheerful smile? Could a smile be joyous, tearful, wholehearted, toothless, toothsome, forced, heart-warming, wavering, fixed, reluctant, etc.? Could a child with a reluctant smile possibly be feeling the same way as a child with a tearful smile, or a timid one? Here are special shades of *happy*:

jubilant, joyous, gay, bubbling, bouncy, sparkling, effervescent, delighted, cheerful, contented, etc.

Here is *sadness* qualified:

mournful, wistful, depressed, downhearted, gloomy, heavy-hearted, melancholy, downcast, sullen, dejected, discouraged, etc.

Phrases of All Kinds

Still another descriptive tool is the little phrase that has the telling action in it. Although they have their place, one must be careful to avoid becoming too dependent on such phrases; sentences can be cumbersome when too many phrases weigh them down. Here are some phrases to give character to the verb *walk:*

he walks
dragging his legs	with head turned to the sky
scuffing his toes	looking neither here nor there
swinging his arms	with boredom on his face
hunched and bent	intently observing
hands in pockets	with an awful clatter

In mentioning the language of the record, it seems as though we are adding more hurdles to the ones teachers already face while taking records. Certainly there are not enough good opportunities for recording, the speed at which one must work is frustrating, and sheer muscular endurance plays its part in the difficulties too. Even though the challenge of using descriptively precise language may be still another hurdle, the problem of good use of language in recording is one we must overcome. We are not accustomed in our culture to being colorful and descriptive in our everyday speech, although we may enjoy such qualities in reading. Nevertheless, records that are truly pictorial are so in large part as a result of imaginative language. If you feel too discouraged, try looking in Roget's *Thesaurus* or the dictionary for synonyms for some of the most commonly used action words and feeling tones. You will be surprised at the number of descriptive words you actually know and can put into your active command with a little joggling.

6

RECORDING CHILDREN'S BEHAVIOR WITH ONE ANOTHER

How Children Learn to Socialize

IT IS perhaps hard to believe, but nevertheless true, that young children at first look at one another as they do at objects and materials—as something to touch, to smell, and maybe to taste! So much is this so, that a little two-year-old pours sand on another child's head and then stares in amazement at his distress, or calmly pushes someone down the stairs if he is in the way, or pokes a finger into a youngster's eye to see what makes it shine. This sounds like the cruelest savagery but it is really nothing more than evidence for the fact that there is a time in the life of every human being when he does not understand that other people have feelings like his own. As a matter of fact, there is even a time when human beings do not understand that they themselves are separate, individual people, capable of independent feeling and action. The consciousness of self, of being somebody, comes gradually. Paradoxically, one must have awareness of this selfness, this being, before one can even suspect that other living creatures feel pain and pleasure.

FEELINGS AND KNOW-HOW

The early years are the ones when attitudes toward people are laid down in the character structure of the child, and the techniques for getting along in our culture are more or less painfully learned. As teachers, we have to be aware of three things about children's social development:

A child's attitudes toward people
(affection, love, trust, suspicion, hate, etc.)

43

The strength of his feelings
  (deep, casual, indifferent)
How much and what kind of know-how he has in getting along
  (Do you get a doll by asking for it, stealing it, or grabbing it?)

In this sense, a child may feel warm and loving to all humanity, but show it crudely, perhaps by hugging those who do not want hugging at the moment. Or a child may be jealous and resentful, but knowing that hugging is approved by adults and hitting is not, he may hug to hurt. By the time a child comes to school, there has already been a complex background of experience shaping his attitudes and techniques. He himself, however, is still very much in the process of learning (as we are too) and quite receptive to our efforts to help him feel wholesome attitudes and practice constructive techniques.

A CHILD BECOMES AWARE OF SELF

When a child is newborn, he is completely unconcerned with other human beings. He becomes conscious of them first in relation to their handling of his needs and wants, which means quite naturally from a self-centered point of view. This is neither wrong nor unnatural. It is, however, the base from which future behavior with people will develop, sooner for some, later for others.

At the time that a child starts to speak of himself as "I" instead of in the third person (e.g., "Stevie wants water"), he is still examining other children with curiosity and interest, but without comprehension. Not until he feels himself a person (he knows his name, his sex, his likes and dislikes, and something of where he belongs), can he look at others and sense "They feel even as I feel." It is natural to the growth of a young child, therefore, to be in a state of progression from non-identification with others toward increasing capacity for sympathy and understanding. Before one can guide a child in social relationships, one must know how far along that child is on the road to maturity.

HOW FAR IS FAR?

When teachers first see them at school, children have not had too much time as yet for maturing. They behave with one another only as they know how within their limits. They may long to please us but still do unto each other only as they know how rather than as we think they should. Even as we show them better techniques for getting along with one another, we must accept without condemnation the inadequate techniques they already have. This does not mean that all and any behavior is permitted to go on without an effort to direct it. To do that would be a real disservice to children because they are dependent on us for the cues to what is socially acceptable. It does mean, however, that we may not expect of children behavior they neither know about nor are capable of performing. So often what we judge to be naughty is due to sheer ignorance.

By the time we reach adulthood we have already incorporated into our personalities the morality and ethics of our culture. Young children, however, are still somewhat uninitiated and much of what they do is meaningful to them only in the purely personal terms of how they feel about what's happening and not in the objective sense of what is right or wrong. Understanding and accepting a child's anger, jealousy, rivalry, fear, ambition, and anxiety establish an atmosphere of acceptance in which he can grow into socially necessary and morally desirable behavior without losing his self-respect and dignity as a human being.

We cannot close the gap between adulthood and childhood by trying to behave like children ourselves. But we can use our imagination and feel with children so that we see what is important to them from the limits of their experience as well as from the breadth of ours.

DO WE REALLY SEE WHAT IS GOING ON?

It is inevitable that teachers will apply their own yardsticks of social right and wrong to children's behavior, and it is good for children to learn from people who have convictions. But we adults have to be reasonably certain that our expectations fit the capacities of the children. We feel sure about what is right and wrong because we learned our lessons well in childhood. It happens that our "intuitive" knowledge is often contradicted by research findings because we learned as children without understanding many of the attitudes we consider "natural" and "right" as adults. Earlier in this manual biases and prejudices that influence interpretations of behavior were discussed. They influence what we see, too, as anyone can testify who has listened to the conflicting testimony of eyewitnesses to an accident.

Biases and prejudices are not necessarily negative or undesirable. But observation and, it follows, interpretations of children's behavior are more likely to be accurate when we know what our particular biases happen to be.

Seeing a child rejected by his peers is for some of us clearly a call to come to the defense, and in we move to demand humane behavior from the little tyrant. For others of us a physical tussle between youngsters is unnerving and perhaps a little frightening. Again we hear the call to action, and with feelings of righteousness mete out justice "impartially." For still others the "show-off," the "bossy type," the "hog," the "poor sport," the "sneak," etc., are children whose behavior does something to us, impelling us to stop them somehow. And stop them we do, not always because it is necessarily right or in the children's best interests, but because we need to quiet the disturbance inside ourselves. We have feelings too. And when children's behavior makes us uncomfortable, we do something to ease the discomfort if we possibly can.

How sure can we be that our techniques for handling anti-social or asocial behavior are the most helpful ones when we ourselves feel personally involved in this way? How sure are we that we are seeing all there is in a situation, and not only the obvious, the dramatic, or that which is personally important?

Do we assume that all smiles mean pleasure and all tears pain? That boisterous, noisy fighting can hurt more than quiet, calculated avoidance? Do we really see what is going on?

What, for example, is happening to the two who are smiling at each other on the swings? Is this a budding friendship of two shy ones or a budding plot of two rascally ones? Just what is going on between the two who hug a corner and engage in endless conversations? Are they seeking each other out for support or for stimulation? Can we always be sure what and who started a fight? Is every fight bad?

We need to ask ourselves whether every child in the group has a friend and whether all the friendships are profitable to those concerned. Do some children need special help from adults in getting along with others? Are there some for whom the best adult guidance is a "hands off" policy?

We must learn to look at children without preconceptions of what they "ought" to be doing, if we want to see what they *are* doing.

CHILDREN ARE DIFFERENT FROM ONE ANOTHER

Some children follow a consistent pattern toward all other children. They are pleasant and sweet-tempered with all comers, always welcoming and accepting and equally gracious with everyone. An opposite kind of consistency is present in the child who is always suspicious, always hostile, a "lone wolf" on his own. How many such completely consistent personalities are there in a group? Not many. We might say that such people, big or little, seem to have something inside them that keeps them one way all the time, regardless of what is happening outside themselves. But most children, like most adults, react to a number of things. One might be the behavior and expectations of the other fellow. A second might be the irritability of coming down with mumps or measles. A third might be the abundance or scarcity of what the child wants. And so on.

A situation can affect children's reactions to one another. The presence or absence of certain teachers or a long spell indoors with no chance for physical activity would be such a situation. Or, on occasion, normally unaggressive children can become aggressive under the cover of group protection, or when they feel unjustly deprived. Some children learn quite early whom they may push with impunity and whom to follow with regard. They sometimes seem to have a sixth sense about the child who is unable to defend himself.

In other words, reactions to people are many-sided, especially while children are still learning the techniques of getting along with others, as is true in the early years. It is no surprise, therefore, that the happy, normal youngster may show different kinds of reactions. If we would guide him to good, successful interpersonal adjustment, we have to be sure that we know what his reactions to others actually are.

Details to Look for in Observing a Child's Behavior with Other Children

Every teacher picks up a lot of useful information out of the corner of her eye as she goes about her busy day. She knows that a combination of Susie and Naomi is sure to end up in mischief; that once started on cowboy play, Kenny, Jim, and Lewis will keep at it for the whole outdoor period; that Jane will probably wander again today as she has since coming to school; and so on.

Is that enough? *Who approached whom* in the Susie-Naomi combination? Who started the cowboy idea? Who leads? Who follows? How do the children make contact with one another?

Some children approach others with certainty and sure-footedness. "Let's play," they say forthrightly, and play it is. Others come along with less assurance. "May I play?" they ask timidly, or hesitantly, or uncertainly. Some children walk up to others and stand speechless, waiting for acceptance and admission to the golden realm. And some wait for no introduction, but direct the activity immediately. "You be my passenger. I'm the driver."

Who approached whom? Is it that way all the time? Are there some children who always have to be asked, and some who never ask? Are children different with different members of the group, asking some and not others, accepting some and not accepting others?

WHO APPROACHED WHOM? HOW DID HE DO IT?

Was he bold and demanding?
Was he friendly and assuring?
Was he frightened and expectant of rebuff?
Did he touch or push?
Did he caress the other child?
Did he gesture at him in some way?
Or did the teacher get the whole thing started?

As a child approaches another child, he may be casual, relaxed, and at ease. He may be friendly or hostile, confident or afraid. He may have the right words or still be relying on body contact. *His approach will show both his attitude and his know-how.*

HOW DOES HE DO WHAT HE DOES?

We get the quality of a child's approach to other children by the quality of his voice, the rhythm and tempo of his speech, his facial expression, and his body movements. They are all there in one integrated response. We react to this total response, of course, but in recording it is necessary to become sensitive to the parts that make up the whole in the interest of greater accuracy.

We have talked before of the difference between WHAT a child does and HOW he does it. It is perhaps even more important to see how a child behaves socially than how he uses materials, because adults are far likelier to take sides and do something when children are working out their social relationships than when they are exploring materials. To see the meaning of the experience to the child, we must be sure to see how he does what he does.

Body positions and movement. Perhaps it is hard for us to pin down and record significant body positions and movements in children because as adults we have become so circumscribed in our own movements that we cannot feel the meaning of theirs in our own bodies. We do not sprawl on the floor easily any more; we don't give way to laughter by flinging our legs over our heads; we don't fall easily; we prefer sitting to running. In short, we have ceased to use our own bodies with the freedom and abandon of children. Consequently, we do not look at a jumping or climbing youngster and tingle in our own muscles with his exhilaration in stretching his limbs. Yet body expression is personality expression. A person's body is himself. He uses it as he feels.

So often children strike first and ask later, or grow rigid with fear but say nothing, or stand with head low and voice mute. The tilt of the head, the use of the hands, body stances, amount of body activity, bodily contacts (touch, shove, push, pat, buck) all are means of communicating. Trust and fear, self-confidence and inadequacy, all find expression in bodily posture. So do restlessness, irritability, composure, and serenity. We know this to be true from experience. We must include the details of body movement in our records.

Quality of voice. This is an integral part of communication. As a child speaks, his emotional state will be revealed in his voice.

> Is it strident, soft, querulous, screechy, flat, pleading?
> Is it lilting, whining, demanding, loud, strained, forceful, quivery?

"Give it to me, he growled" is hardly the same expression of feeling as "Give it to me, he whined petulantly."

Tempo and rhythm. These qualities of a child's speech tell us something about the tempo and rhythm of *him.* He may drawl and move in unhurried fashion, or his words may tumble in unending floods of ideas and feeling. Slowness or speed may simply be the result of the organization of the child's nervous system (as it usually is), but it may be the result of anxiety too. A child slows up when he is afraid of saying the "wrong thing." He hurries when he's afraid he won't be listened to. Fast, slow, moderate—these refer to tempo. Rhythm is something else again. Rhythm is smoothness, jerkiness, or hesitancy. The rhythm of speech can be staccato, cadenced, or flowing. Combining tempo and rhythm, we find that a child's speech can be fast and smooth or fast and jerky, slow and even or slow and hesitant. Rhythm and tempo together characterize the quality of the speech.

Facial expression. This accompanies "quality" in speech. We expect smiling eyes with laughter, a droopy mouth with tears. Here are some of the descriptive terms we can use:

Eyes can be solemn, glaring, flashing, tearful, smiling, sleepy, bright, shiny, dull, sparkling, etc.

Mouth can be drooping, smiling, pouting, quivering, laughing, puckered, drawn, lips curled over teeth, etc.

Smile can be wholehearted, uncertain, full, wistful, furtive, reluctant, shy, open, dimpled, and half!

Of course not all details appear in every record. For one thing, no child uses his entire battery of possible shades of expression every time he reacts to life. For another, no human recorder could see enough or write fast enough to get everything onto a piece of paper. But the more details you can record that point to what is happening inside a child as he makes his contact, the more accurate and expressive will be the picture that emerges.

. . . . .

Sandy shaded her eyes with her hands, frowned, and stared across the yard at Lillian. Her under lip jutted forward in a pout and her brows furrowed deeper than ever. Suddenly she swung her hands into fists at her side, stamped her foot and exploded. "Hey!" She ran across the yard and grabbed Lillian by the arm. Her head punctuated every word as she screamed into Lillian's face, "Who told you to take my umbrella out of my locker?"

. . . . .

Edith slithered silently against the wall, slowly edging her way from the clothing lockers to the clay table. She stood still some two feet away, sober and unsmiling, eyes darting from side to side as she followed the conversation being tossed around the table. Norman looked up and saw Edith. "Hi," he grinned, "Hi, Edie." Still standing immobile, Edith's face crinkled into a warm, open smile. Her eyes alive, shining, she chirped, "Hi, Normie."

. . . . .

WHAT DOES THE CHILD SAY? HOW DOES THE OTHER CHILD RESPOND?

Speech may not reveal everything, but it tells a good deal. Record the actual words as far as possible and not just the sense of what a child says.

"Hey, Pete, let's put the big one here."
"Naw, it'll fall off."
"No it won't, no it won't."
"O.K." (good-naturedly).
"Push that one back a little."
No answer.
"Hey!" (sharply) "Push that one back."

Does it take longer to write the actual dialogue than to write a paragraph about dialogue? The conversation above could be written about as follows:

Tony told Pete where to put the blocks. Pete was pretty agreeable. When Pete didn't answer, Tony shouted at him.

The first is raw material. It is flavorful and authentic and, more important, uninterpreted. The second may be accurate as to interpretation, but it involves the teacher's appraisal of the situation. Should she be wrong, there is no going back to check.

Approaching someone is only part of the relationship. After that, the other person's response or lack of response determines further action. What does the other child do and say? How does he do it? The record quoted above about Edith, though short, is a clear-cut illustration of how behavior is affected by other persons' responses.

WHAT HAPPENS NEXT?

After a contact is made, then what does a child do? Is there a sigh of relief and a quiet settling down to blissful submission? Is there a staccato-like bidding for supremacy of ideas and position? Or is there a purr of contentment as alternatives are weighed with other children? Do the children carry on conversation? Play the same thing separately? If the contact ends without going on into dramatic play, tell how it ends and what the child does immediately after. His subsequent behavior may reflect his feelings about the contact.

If the contact blossoms into dramatic play, as it so often does, there are new and additional considerations. These can best be understood if we recognize that children project themselves into their play and work out problems both of intellectual comprehension ("Is steering a bus different from steering a plane?") and of emotional complexity ("I want what I want now, but if I say so, Stevie may go away"). Mostly, dramatic play is fun, and deeply satisfying fun at that. But it is also the children's way of exploring the meaning of activities and relationships in the grown-up world. It is learning to get along with other children, to share and bargain, to compare and evaluate, to compete and cooperate, to give and take. At the same time, the magic of "make-believe" allows children to work out their wishes, aspirations, and fears and their other childhood fantasies. All this they do by playing a part, a *role*, in dramatic play. The role is compounded of bits from the real world and pieces from inside themselves. Bits and pieces do not always make a logical whole in the eyes of an adult, and that is perhaps why children's play often seems inconsequential, irrational, or delightfully fluid and without boundaries.

But play has logic to children, and the strongest evidence of this is the amount of dramatic play that goes on all through childhood. Even children who hardly know each other slip into the world of imagination together, understanding each other hardly at all in our sense, but speaking the language of dramatic play.

Recording a Child's Behavior in Dramatic Play

After noting the *setting* (outdoors, doll-corner, on the jungle-gym, etc.) and how the contact was made, indicate the *course of action*, or sequence of events, including the dialogue. Into the sequence of events, weave the roles assumed by the children, and *how* the roles are played.

A dramatic role has many facets. For example, (1) there is the role itself, its content; (2) a child's position in relation to the others playing; (3) the emotional investment in the role; (4) the reactions of others to the child. Let us look at each of these in detail.

THE ROLE ITSELF, ITS CONTENT

Ideas come from the tangible world of reality.

people—father, mother, engineer, baby, storekeeper, captain, sister, maid, fireman, policeman, beauty-parlor operator, etc.

inanimate objects—train, airplane, truck, doll, etc.

By reproducing aspects of the real world which he has experienced, or longs to experience, a child tries to fix in his mind their properties, processes, and relationships. He includes that which to his mind and limited experience is the meaningful quality and character of the person or thing. And how accurately children pinpoint the essence of train, plane, animal, or parent in terms of outstanding action, sound, or feeling value! It takes them longer to see and understand technical details, the parts of the whole, ramifications, complexity, variety, etc. This kind of evidence gathered in dramatic play can be used by teachers to assess intellectual awareness or confusion of children. This knowledge in turn furnishes a base for planning experiences that increase or clarify children's conceptions of the real world. We must be careful, however, not to jump to conclusions. A child may be sitting on what looks like a train and not give us a hint as to whether he is the engineer, the train itself, a passenger, or the cargo!

This record of dramatic play shows the content of the role the child is playing.

Four-year-old Alfred went straight to the blocks when he came to the nursery. There were only two other children at school at the time, both at the clay table. Alfred started to build what looked like a train. He set five blocks in a long row on the floor. At one end he put two blocks on top of each other and sat on them. Danny had just come in and walked over to Alfred.

Danny. "Is that a bridge?"

Alfred. "No, it's a train."

"Where's it going?"

"To New York. I'm the engineer. I build big trains."

"I'm conductor. I drive the train."

Alfred, impatiently, "No, no. I'm the engineer. I made it."

Danny. "What can I do?"

"You collect the tickets."

"What tickets?"

Alfred. "The ones the passengers give you . . . (out loud) Who wants a ride on the train? . . . All abo-a-rd . . . All ab-o-oard. Train going. Woo . . . woo . . . It goes so fast."

Harry came into the room and ran over to the train.

Harry. "I want to get on." He got another block from the shelf and put it on the middle of the train. He picked up a very small block from the floor and held it to his mouth as he would a telephone and yelled, "Hello, hello. What's wrong with you? We're leaving and we gotta have food. Bring hundreds of boxes. . . . Right away, you hear?" He slammed the telephone down.

Alfred. "We got a flat. I'll fix it. Got to fix it now." With swaggering pretentiousness he removed one of the blocks from the line and turned it upside down and replaced it. Then he got back on the two blocks.

Mitchell came over and got on the train.

Alfred. "Get off, get off. It's my train. . . . (demandingly) GO AWAY."

He gave Mitchell a push to get him off. Mitchell attempted to get on again, and again Alfred pushed him off. The teacher complimented Alfred on his train and suggested that he allow other children to share it with him. Alfred made no response, but did nothing when Mitchell got on again and sat behind him.

Alfred. "No gas, no gas. Hey, Mitch, no gas. Ha, Ha! Now no gas. First flat tire, now no gas."

Danny took the block which Harry had used as a telephone and called on it. "Hey, you. Bring gas. Train needs gas. Ha! Ha! Hurry up, you dope."

Alfred. "All off! It's lunch time. Let's get some food. Follow me. I'll show you, men."

. . . . .

A CHILD'S POSITION IN RELATION TO THE OTHERS PLAYING

As the members of a group interact, they tend to find spots for themselves in the group's hierarchy and structure. Some children are leaders, some followers, some peacemakers, and some moralists representing the adult's point of view. Some children barely fit into the group as legitimate members at all.

A child's position in the group may be obvious or subtly concealed and disguised. A child who seems to be a cooperator may just be a slavey in disguise. Eagerness to be accepted, anxiety about what he has to offer may lead him to a fairly thorough denial of his right to a genuinely cooperative position. The child who is noisiest in a group may seem to be the leader and yet the real direction may be coming from a quiet youngster who controls the play by force of ideas. Position in the group is one of the important components of interrelating. For one youngster leadership may be so important that he will resort to any trick he can think up to reach his goal. For another there may be quiet contentment in not being challenged. Position has two faces— how the adult sees a child's position in the group, and how the child himself sees it and feels about it.

> Position could be boss, constructive leader, cooperative member, fringer, compromiser, etc.
>
> Position can be maintained by bullying, force of ideas, persuasion, reasoning, coaxing, bribing, silence, force, etc.

Here is a record of three boys who long to challenge the position of a fourth.

Barry, Paul and Ben have congregated on one side of the play yard, heads together. Teacher hears Barry, in conspiratorial tones, "That Max hits! I'll do something so he can't catch me. Know what?"

Ben's eyes widen and he asks interestedly, "No—what?"

Barry draws himself up imperiously. He smiles in roguish fashion and announces loudly, "I'll kill him." He glances up and sees the teacher.

"Know why we're here, Mrs. K.?"

T. "No. why?"

Barry triumphantly pulls the other boys back and points to a small bush they have been surrounding.

"There are prickles on these branches." (Sure enough, there are still some sticky burrs on the bush.) Barry hastily strips them off the branches and distributes them.

"Here. Here. Now we each have one, we're going to throw them at people."

Ben is dancing up and down in anticipation. "We're bad guys," he shouts, "we'll fool everyone."

Paul has been standing, brow creased, holding his burr gingerly. Still frowning, he speaks deliberately. "Max Evans throws sand at us, let's throw at Max Evans."

Barry hops on one foot, his eyes dancing. "He won't see us. We'll tell him to look at something else."

They take off, Paul and Ben well in the lead. Barry brings up the rear.

Max and his cohorts are at the other side of the play yard busy on a project of their own. The three boys approach by a circuitous route, going more slowly as they come closer. Then at a signal from Ben, they fire their burrs in what they hope is Max's direction. They are all well out of retaliatory range, yelling, "I've got you!" As Max takes a step in their direction they scatter, shouting, "Run, run!" Max doesn't follow, but turns to his friends, saying, "See, they're scared."

· · · · ·

EMOTIONAL INVESTMENT IN THE ROLE

As a child plays a dramatic part, such as doctor, mother, baby, captain, etc., he may give that part an emotional quality and tone that is deeply personal.

He may play the role in terms of his feelings and attitudes toward other children.
(even though he is storekeeper, mother, or fireman, he might be domineering, bossy, timid, conscientious, kind, forceful, subservient, tyrannical, protective, etc.)

He may act out areas of feeling not otherwise revealed.
How he thinks people feel toward each other
(the doctor may be kind, brusque, or scolding; mothers and fathers may be kind, brusque, or scolding)

How he wishes people would behave toward him
(a father is understanding, forceful, positive, kind, a friend, etc.; a brother is a giving, helping person, a pal, etc.)

How he would express himself if it were permissible
(he plays the baby so he can pretend he is protected and dependent; he becomes a tiger so that he can growl with impunity; he plays father so that he can dominate; etc.)

All these attitudes could be consistent in his play, and he would then always be tyrannical or always kind, whether father, captain, policeman, or uncle. But it is just as likely that attitudes will change with the role, as well as with different people. He could be subservient to a big, strong fellow, but high-handed with the girls. We have to observe a child at dramatic play more than once, and with many children, to see which behavior is characteristic of his relations with others.

REACTIONS OF OTHERS TO THE CHILD

Children test and modify the effectiveness of their social attitudes and techniques via the responses of others. Position, status, or acceptance for any child is dependent not only on his actions, but on the willingness of other children to see him in terms suitable to his own concepts of what he is like and what he wants. The teacher who would help a child achieve more mature social behavior must know the impact of children on each other in two ways: objectively (this is what happened); and in the subjective meaning to the youngster involved (what he thought happened).

> Which children react?
> What do they do? How do they do it?
> What do they say? How do they say it?
> Do they fit in with his plans, use him, resist, follow him under protest, etc?

As you complete the recording, be sure to indicate how the play ends. Leaving a group can have as many implications as entering it.

> Does the child leave for some other play?
> Does the other child (or children) leave him?
> Does the teacher interrupt the play? (for juice, pick-up, etc.)
> Does it develop into some other kind of play?
> How long did the child's participation last?

In this record, the child's position in the group, his feelings about maintaining that position, and the reactions of others seem quite clear.

Several little groups of youngsters were scattered through the wooded area of the play yard, some digging, some filling cans, some using a rock for the dinner table in their imaginary home. Peter and cohorts had used cans to collect items for dinner, then to gather maple syrup (sap) from the trees. Peter left his cans by a tree and came swinging past Denise's rock.

P. "I'm going to get my fishing cast and go out in the boat. Mama, (addressing Denise) will you row the boat for me while I'm fishing?" Peter did not wait for an answer but continued on his quest for his fishing rod. From far away he called. "Come on, Mama!"

Denise was adamant. "I need to make the lunch at home on the stove!"

Peter found a long rod-like pole and returning, paused again by Denise.

P. "Come on, Mama. Now you be careful making that lunch." He strode toward his boat rock. "Come on, Mama. Come on, we have to go. You have to row . . . That's the boat house and you come with me."

Denise kept on with her lunch-making, but called after Peter, "Good-by!"

Peter was now back on his rock, his fishing rod stowed aboard. He stood there holding onto a tree branch, looking across the woods to Denise and calling. Impatience at being balked was beginning to creep into his tone.

P. "Come on! You have to row for me."

D. "You go on. I can't do it."

P. screaming, "Come on! *You have to do it!*"

With each word he beat the branch with a short stick for emphasis and to give vent to his feelings since he couldn't beat Denise, but probably would have liked to rush over and do so.

D. in a disgruntled, placating voice, "All right. Let me finish the onions. Bring the children. Come on, Louise." So she and her companion moved over to the boat.

Peter now had Stephen, Leslie, Robert, Denise, and Louise on the rock-boat. He was using a stick for an oar. Then he saw Nancy and Julie busy digging. (New fields to conquer!)

P. "Come on, sisters. (to N. and J.) Will you row for us, sisters?" They came easily. But soon Julie was in tears. Denise was slapping her hands hard for dumping dirt from her can and getting the boat dirty.

P. "Stop that, Denise!"

Julie got off the boat and went away, spirits wounded, head bent. Louise edged in next to Peter on the rock.

P. "That's where Mama's going to sit. Now get out." He pushed her away so Denise could come. Denise took up Peter's long stick.

P. "Stop! That's my fishing cast!"

Denise got off the boat, found herself a long fishing rod, and returned.

P. to Leslie, "Brother, will you row?" Leslie refused.

P. looking around, "Well, who's going to row?" Spying Denise with her own fishing rod, "Mama, you row. We only want one fishing cast. Look! I caught a big one (a leaf at the end of his stick). *Listen,* who's going to row? (to Denise) Mama, you go over there, and fish over there. It's the nicest place on the boat. Now, boy (to Leslie), row with this stick." Having at last made someone row, he turned to his fishing.

· · · · ·

Résumé of Details of a Single Episode

Taken all together, the significant aspects of a record of a child making a contact with another child might fall into some such general outline as the following.

1. Setting
   Where does the contact take place?
   What were the children doing before the contact was made?

2. How is the contact made?
> What does the child who initiated the contact do? What does he say?
>
> Did the teacher get the whole thing started? How?
>
> How does the child do what he does?
>> Body positions and movement
>>
>> Quality of voice
>>
>> Tempo and rhythm of speech
>>
>> Facial expression
>
> How does the other child respond? What does the other child say?

3. What happens next? In recording a child's behavior during dramatic play, be sure to include
>> Dialogue
>>
>> Content of the dramatic role the child is playing
>>
>> Position in the group
>>
>> Emotional investment in the role
>>
>> Reaction of others to him

4. How does the play end?
> What or who seems responsible for the ending?
>
> How do the children disperse?
>
> What is the feeling tone? (happy, guilty, despairing, belligerent, contented, etc.)

Patterns of Behavior

Out of such details as those above there will emerge *patterns of behavior,* or the characteristic way in which a child is likely to respond in his relations with children. Over a period of a school year, *changing* patterns indicate growth or regression. We can organize these patterns of behavior by clustering items from the single episodes around such categories as the following:

1. Evidence of interest in children
> Direct evidence would be the number of children played with; or a child's request for help in entering play situations; or positive approaches to children.
>
> Indirect evidence would be staring at others or watching them; imitating; attempting to attract attention from children by various means.

2. How are contacts made?
> Does the child move toward others or against them? (initially, or always)

How does he move? (confidently, tentatively, pleadingly, timidly, aggressively, etc.)

Do others move toward him, away from, or against him? (initially or always)

How does he react to the behavior of others? (to their affection, invitation to play, criticism, suggestions and ideas, aggressions, etc.)

What does he do?

(withdraws, enters play, rejects, tolerates, defies, aggresses, complains to adults, etc.)

How does he do it?

(shyly, confidently, eagerly, with curiosity and interest, crying, angrily, happily, fearfully, etc.)

What methods does he use in making contacts?

(speech, attack, with ideas, with things, enters situation directly, threatens, bribes, uses others to gang up, asks adults for help, etc.)

3. How does he behave with children?

To what extent can he make his wishes, desires, irritations, annoyances, ideas, etc., understood?

To what extent is he able to share equipment, props, materials?

To what extent is he able to await his turn?

What are the more usual causes of clashes with others? (possessions, ideas, unprovoked attacks, etc.)

How does he handle conflicts?

What does he do?

(runs to teacher, cries, fights back, reasons, jokes, etc.)

How does he do it?

(tearfully, righteously, sobbing, angrily, indignantly, etc.)

To what extent is he aware of others' rights and needs?

How realistic are his demands for his own rights?

How does he protect his rights?

To what extent does he seek help from other children?

(how, under what circumstances, from whom)

To what extent is he able to help others?

(how, when, and whom)

To what extent does he contribute ideas, suggestions?

Does he accept other people's ideas, suggestions?

Does his desire for status, prestige, affection, or attention interfere with the progress of the play situation?

What is his general tone at play—amiable, hostile, creating dissension?

What seem to be his defense mechanisms?

4. What seem to be his feelings about other children?
   (likes, fears, envies, etc.)
   Special friends (how many and who; nature of interrelation-
      ships)

5. Where does he fit in relation to entire group?
   Does he play with none, one, many, both sexes?
   Is he an established member of group; is he making his way;
      is he a lone player?
   How does he act toward new children entering the group?

6. What *roles* does he take in dramatic play?
   (engineer, father, mother, baby, animal, train, etc.)

7. In playing roles, as above, what *position* does he take in relation
   to others?
   (Although playing such roles as mother, baby, or engineer,
   his *position* is that of boss, subordinate, leader, cooperator,
   moralist, scapegoat, etc.)

   Does he always assume one position or is it only in relation to
      certain personalities, i.e., is he always the boss or only with
      the timid children? (younger ones, older, boys, girls, aggressive
      children, etc.)

   How is his position maintained?
   (by the enticement of ideas, by rationalizing, talking excessively, reasoning, humor, aggression—verbal as well as physical, threats, bribery, under protest, by helplessness, etc.)

8. Special problems or trends
   (impatience with others; letting himself be exploited by others;
   excessive hitting, temper, or withdrawal; lack of speech; other
   physical handicaps; excessive dependence on teacher; different
   cultural background from group's; etc.)

9. Evidences of growth
   Comparison of earlier and later behavior indicating more
      mature level

Summing up the generalizations that seem reasonable in light of the
patterns that emerge out of the wealth of detail, we bring into focus
an image of how a very much alive, vibrant child reacts in one important area of living. On the basis of such evidence we shall eventually be able to form hypotheses, and plan for action. Judgment will
have been based on objective data. Generalizations about two children's relationships with others follow.

Records of Children's Behavior with Other Children

Jimmy, age 4:

Jimmy has always shown a great interest in the other children and their activities. He used to stand watching them at their work a great deal. But if they looked his way, he would turn away and drop his head. He made no effort to contact anyone. At first the children ignored him pretty much. It was not until he began to help me serve juice that they even seemed aware of him at all.

The two children who seemed to fascinate Jimmy most were Lenny and Martha. Both four-year-olds, they are quick, active children, hopping from one thing to another. Good friends, they laugh and sing all day. Jimmy began to follow them around after being at school about two months. He would laugh at their antics until they began to use him as their special audience. Some time later they began to draw him into their play, giving him the role of baby or dog or anything else which they themselves preferred not to be. Jimmy, not being aggressive, fell into these roles and played them to the limit, delighted at being included.

The other children now seem to accept Jimmy as Lenny and Martha's friend and apparently like him. Although he never initiates play, we notice that he is not always willing to play baby any more. He seems to avoid rough-and-tumble, stepping aside if he sees it near him. He rarely joins in a group, but will now play with two or three children he knows well.

. . . . .

Lee, age 4 yrs. 5 mo.:

With his peers Lee shows a pattern of caution, observing them closely before he joins them. It has just been during the past few weeks that he has taken part in singing and rhythmic group activities. He seems to derive great satisfaction from this type of activity, asking, "Are we going to play the Jingle Bell game today?" etc. If sufficiently absorbed in a certain task he ignores others in his immediate vicinity completely. He is friendly with most children, but tends to seek out one particular child to play with. This child changes on a day-to-day or week-to-week basis. When a third child enters (in my notes, it seems always to be Michael) he feels very insecure, covering his feelings of hostility with a sulky withdrawal, seldom with an overt act of aggression. (This week I did see him pounce unexpectedly upon Michael's back and wrestle him to the floor with much triumphant laughter on his part and complete bewilderment on Michael's.) Although Lee talks a great deal he seems to be talking at the children most times, not with them. They all delight in listening to his tall stories. He has a good sense of humor and his hearty laugh can be heard throughout the room. He often uses laughter as a release from tension.

Just lately Lee has shown signs of approaching readiness to take aggressive action (e.g., wrestling Michael and Paul). His mother reported that he has told her proudly at home, "I had a big fight and I made that kid almost cry." Actually it was a very little fight, but its importance to Lee in his self-picture is very evident.

7

THE CHILD'S RELATIONSHIPS WITH ADULTS

CHILDREN are born helpless, and for a long time they remain largely dependent on adults. Yet, to reach mature adulthood, they must somehow make the transition to relative independence. This they accomplish in many steps and stages, sometimes obviously and dramatically, sometimes with quiet ease. The struggle for independence is not waged without qualms and fears on the part of the child. While he is breaking the bonds, he continues to need the adult, not only for physical sustenance, affection, and understanding but for moral support in this drive to independence.

From the adults who are most important in his early years, his parents, he learns many things. His concepts of people and what to expect of them and his concept of himself and what he may or may not do are shaped by the daily contacts with these significant adults. He believes that all adults are like the ones he first knew well until long years of experience beyond early childhood teach him to recognize differences. He believes that what they tell him about himself is true, unless other people later teach him otherwise. Consequently, when a child enters school for the first time, his behavior with teachers will in large measure reflect his home experience and indicate how far along the road to full independence he has gone.

Observation of a child's relationship with adults as we see it revealed at school can tell us whether the child feels that adults are to be trusted, or viewed with suspicion; whether they are to be exploited for one's own ends, hated fiercely, or avoided. We can tell, too, whether the child believes he can run the gamut of human feeling from best to worst, break adult taboos of right and wrong, and still remain loved; or whether he thinks he must carefully refrain from doing anything that will offend adult standards and thus cause him to lose adult love.

64

The details of the adult-child relationship will, in many instances, be an incidental part of the situations dealt with up to now, i.e., the child's functioning during routines, with materials, or in relation to children. In addition, however, there are special adult-child contacts, as every teacher knows, because she herself is involved.

There is the time a child grabs one's hand and squeezes it, or catapults out of the doorway and forcefully leaps onto us by way of morning greeting; there is the quiet moment of confidence when a child brings a worm for inspection or holds up a wet nose to be wiped; there is the imperious demand for attention, the teasing and the shared laughter. Every day brings new relationships with the individuals who make up the group. Every child feels he is special in the eyes of his teacher and makes his "special" contacts with her. (If he doesn't, it is worthy of note.)

Details to Look for in Recording a Child's Contact with an Adult

Setting in which the episode takes place
Who makes the contact?
    If the child makes the contact—
        Is it purposeful?
            (child asks for help, asks for materials, shows his products, asks for comfort when hurt—actual or imagined, seeks help at routines, asks to be played with, etc.; bestows affection or asks for it; asks help in social relationships, ideas)
        Is it indirectly purposeful?
            (child seeks attention by excessive talking, by a stream of presents, by provocative activity done deliberately with awareness that it is not acceptable, such as screaming, dangerous climbing, breakage, hiding things, etc.)
    If the teacher makes the contact, what is her purpose?
        (to give assistance with materials or equipment, settle a dispute, enter the play, make suggestions or requests, give directions or orders, give comfort following injury or insult, offer props, etc.)
    What attitude and feeling are revealed by the child as evidenced by his voice, tempo of speech, facial expression, body positions and movement, body contacts?
Dialogue (direct quote)
Sequence of events
    Include what adult does and says.

Indicate child's responses, both verbal and bodily.

How does the contact end?

What does the child do immediately after?

Patterns of Behavior

These are two children who reveal different approaches to a teacher.

Sharon, very blond, pale complexion, blue eyes, flat pug nose and mouth slightly open, arrives at school each morning with her mother. She walks up the path expressionless, almost dragging her legs. Looking around slowly, she heads toward the teacher. The teacher calls, "Hi, Sharon!" but does not receive a response. She calls again, "Hi, Sharon!" and this time receives a faint smile. Sharon maneuvers toward the swings, where one child is already swinging. Sharon wraps herself around the pole and waits. The other child, paying no attention to Sharon, gets off, and Sharon, still moving slowly, eases herself on and begins to pump. Once again she has a slight smile. After a few minutes, she begins to play in the mud, working seriously by herself. She looks up blankly and sees another child bring his finished mud cake to the teacher. The teacher tastes enthusiastically. Still staring, Sharon slowly stands up, and walks over to the teacher, carrying the mud pie carefully. Holding the dish, she stands motionless and speechless for several moments. Then, not saying a word, she turns and sluggishly moves away.

. . . . .

Picking-up time and teacher is cleaning tables. Martha comes over. "I can count to ten," she offers confidentially. "I'd like to hear you," says the teacher, scrubbing away. Hopping on one foot, Martha slowly and accurately counts from one to ten, holding her arms out all the time to help her keep balance. She gives the teacher a smile, all front teeth and crinkled eyes, jumps on two feet and runs off.

. . . . .

Summary of a Child's Relationships with Adults

A summary of a child's relationships with adults can be drawn from many areas of school living, such as casual adult-child contacts throughout the day (what he says and does); the relationship at routines and while using materials and equipment; and through the roles (and the meaning given to them) adopted during dramatic play.

1. How frequently does the child make contact with the adult and in what situations?

(routines; coming for approval, help in conflicts, with materials, ideas, etc.; to give or get affection, be comforted; express hostility; involve adult in his play, seek attention, directly or indirectly; etc.)

Is there a special quality in his contacts with adults?

(whining; demanding; trusting; coy; timid; belligerent; clinging; openly hostile; matter-of-fact, warmhearted; reserved; etc.)

What are his special mechanisms for gaining attention?

(excessive talking; tattling; showing clothes, toys, products, bruises; bringing presents; telling about family; sidling up and touching, hanging on, etc.)

2. How does child react to teacher participation in his life when the teacher is a *giving* person?

When she offers affection—

(child returns it; looks uncomfortable; squirms; seems startled; stiffens up; becomes effusive and gushy; rejects offering; etc.)

When she offers help—

(child accepts it as his right; becomes clingy and helpless; brushes it away; becomes angry; discusses; becomes interested in procedures; etc.)

When she offers suggestions—

(child follows through reluctantly, eagerly; ignores; is grateful; follows through mechanically; rejects; discusses; questions; etc.)

The summary of a child's total response to the teacher as a *giving* person would indicate:

His dependency on this adult (and probably all adults)
His rejection of this adult (and possibly all adults)
His ability to meet adults on equal terms, both to accept and reject the adults' overtures as appropriate

3. How does child react to teacher participation in his life when the teacher is a controlling, inhibiting person, curtailing child's actions and feelings?

When limits are set down, such as group rules and/or personal denial—

(child defies openly; resists passively by lingering, slowing up, remaining at another task; etc.; accepts with overseriousness; accepts with no emotional investment; accepts with a verbalization of the reason; accepts and repeats instructions with parrot-like insistence)

When criticism is given—
(child cries; pouts; accepts cheerfully; shows interest; becomes belligerent; sulks; etc.)

The summary of a child's total responses to the adult as an authority figure would show him as someone who either

Always does as he is told; to whom following adult direction seems more important than his own ideas; has a consistent pattern of subordination to adult ideas and wishes—is compliant, or
Resists authority by any one of a number of patterns, by defiance, questioning, or indifference, or
Finds a balance between carrying out his own independent ideas and wishes and accepting reasonable restrictions.

4. How does he react to sharing the adult with other children, or with other adults?
Teacher helping other children; teacher talking to another teacher or parent; teacher directing the entire group in an activity (story, game, trip, rhythms, explanations, etc.)
(child accepts easily; ignores; interrupts and demands attention; sulks; cries; has tantrums; waits for adults to return to him; awaits his turn patiently but not resignedly)

5. Evidences of growing independence from adults, as seen in
Routines, use of materials, relationships with children, identification with children rather than with adults (perhaps even against adults)

6. Direct verbal expressions

7. Special problems
Overdependence
Excessive insistence on independence
Fear of new adults
Persistent hostility to adults
Excessive displays toward adults, including strangers

Records of Children's Behavior with Adults

The first two months Jimmy was at school, he seemed to need a lot of reassurance from the teacher that he was doing the right thing. He seldom talked, but would raise his eyes questioningly, as if to say, "Is this all right?" With a nod and a smile from her, he would take paper and crayon, or some other material, and proceed to work. But again and again he would seek the teacher out with his eyes. After finishing any work, he would always walk slowly and proudly to the teacher and say, "See, it's for my mommy!" Since he often wandered out into the hall leading into the kitchen, the teacher asked him one day if he would like to accompany her to get the juice. He nodded enthusiastically and walked faster than usual down the hall and into the kitchen. There he struck up the beginning of his friendship with the cook. He remarked to her after a few minutes of observation, "I like it here. What are we going to eat?" After that, Jimmy accompanied the teacher into the kitchen every morning, and he would talk to the cook as the juice was being prepared.

Jimmy seems drawn to any visiting adults and will always edge his way slowly and cautiously to their side, usually displaying something he has made for approval and appreciation. For a long time he just smiled and dropped his head if spoken to. But by now he has gained enough courage to tell his name and age if asked. He is very happy if they praise his work and lingers near until they leave.

. . . . .

At the beginning of the year it was evident that Susie was embarrassed by any attention shown her by adults, except in the routine of help with clothing or toilet. She showed this by her posture, gestures, voice, facial expression, and jerky movement of her body. Next came her bid for attention by loud and excessive talking, laughing, antics, climbing performances, and pretended inability to dress herself (this last in spite of the fact that in the beginning she never needed help with dressing with the exception of placing a garment into proper position). At present she is still behaving in this attention-demanding way, but not as frequently as she has. She comes to show us her dresses (she usually wears overalls), asks to pass out items when need arises. She also seeks help in toileting. Help is not actually needed, but she apparently wants the presence of the teacher in the room.

. . . . .

Young children need adults but they must also gradually loosen the ties. Teachers must be able to observe the relationship in which they are themselves involved with enough dispassionate interest to see the child's dependency needs with objectivity, and see his denial of dependence with realistic and unbiased appraisal. It is perhaps easier to do this if we ask ourselves about a relationship with a child, "Do I enhance or detract from this child's sense of his own powers?" It is hard to be oneself and the impartial observer at the same time. Our professional selves (objective and educated) must become one with our personal selves (subjective and emotionally involved).

8

THE CHILD IN THE GROUP—TEACHER-DIRECTED ACTIVITIES

How ready for music, trip, or story must a child be before the pleasures in such a group activity can have meaning? How grown up to enjoy sharing a common experience with friends? It's one thing to be yourself and get along with others at your own speed. It's another to become an anonymous someone and be moved with a group as an integrated part of it! A child wonders whether to listen for the adult's directions and try to please her or to listen to the cues the children give and seek to be acceptable to them. For most young children, the group situation offers some challenges toward adjustment. The one-to-one relationship established with parents is still very meaningful, and young children vary in the degree to which they can function comfortably outside close and intimate adult-child interaction. A child's response when the group is directed as a group may therefore be quite different from his response when the teacher speaks to him directly or alone.

For one thing, in teacher-directed group activities, the teacher speaks to any one child only by inference, because she speaks to all the children at once in a group. (This is often the reason why young children do not respond to requests given to the group as a whole for clean-up, dressing, etc.) For another, the obvious and compelling competition for the teacher's attention may affect a child's feelings about a group activity to the point where his behavior will be influenced. If he is more concerned about the teacher's favor than about the story, for example, he may respond to the most appealing tale by squirming and wriggling as he pushes and edges his way closer to the beloved adult.

Or, his very ability to perform may be affected by the overwhelm-

70

ing presence of non-indulgent peers, because comparisons are all too often offered by them, and this is not always easy to tolerate. The group situation established by the teacher (i.e., everybody will do the same thing) may therefore be a challenge to a child that is quite different from the looser group situation in which his individual behavior is more closely related to his own desires and wants and not as immediately bounded by peer involvement. Behavior in a teacher-directed activity may thus have its own meaning to a child, quite unrelated to the intent of the teacher.

Any school activity may be reminiscent to a child of his experience in his outside-of-school life, and this will influence his behavior in the group too. For example, if listening to a story at home is enjoyed as much for snuggling next to an adult as for the story itself, how well can a youngster listen at school, removed from physical contact with the teacher and sharing her with a lot of other youngsters? Or, if a child has been struggling secretly to conquer skipping, or jumping with two feet, or hopping, he may not yet be able to prance unself-consciously at rhythms with his better coordinated peers. And it is easy to understand the panic some children undergo as they start across the floor and feel themselves swamped by the stampede of galloping bodies all around them!

Recording Teacher-Directed Activities

Rhythms, trips, and stories are exciting stimuli. Is every child getting the most out of them? In observing a child at any teacher-organized activity, we look for the general child-to-group and child-to-adult relationships as well as to the specifics of the activity. Here, for example, are suggestive details to observe in rhythms.

RHYTHMS—DETAILS TO LOOK FOR IN A SINGLE EPISODE

Child's initial reaction to the announcement that the activity is about to begin
> Positive
>> (eager, joyful, immediate discontinuing of previous activity, etc.)
> Negative
>> (continues with previous activity, dawdles, refuses, complains, runs away, etc.)
> Accepting
>> (compliant, goes along in a matter-of-fact way, etc.)

Sequence of events (content of rhythms period, e.g., singing, rhythmic movement, dramatization, band, etc.)

What does the child do if he participates?

Coordination, special abilities

(walking on toes, running, galloping, skipping, jumping, hopping, creeping, etc.)

Does he respond with body movement (or instruments or clapping) to the rhythm of the music being played?

(i.e., marching in tempo, galloping, etc.)

Does he maintain a rhythm of his own at variance with the rhythm being played?

How does he use the space?

(sweeps the room, stays in one spot, likes to jump up, etc.)

Sense of direction

(Does he move with or against the others? Does he seem confused as to which way to go?)

Creativity, originality, imitativeness

(What does he do that is uniquely his own?)

What are the quality and spirit of his movement?

(lusty, strong, dainty, graceful, bouncy, earth-bound, loose, disjointed, tense, relaxed, tight, restrained, uninhibited, swinging, sweeping, etc.)

Facial expression

Feelings about being "first"

Willingness or unwillingness to do things alone

What does the child do if he does not participate?

(observes group, disrupts, clings to teacher, turns back on group, does something else, runs out of room, etc.)

Place within the group

What position, or social role, does he seem to play?

(leader, follower, disrupter, uses group to hide, etc.)

What status does he have?

How frequently is he chosen by other children (e.g., in games)?

Part played by the adult

(shows children how to move; keeps children from bumping into each other; plays an instrument, etc.)

While the above is specifically related to rhythms, this kind of observation can be applied to other group activities, such as stories, discussions, listening to records, going on trips, or even proceeding from one part of the building to another. The following records reveal two very different kinds of response to typical group situations, music time and rhythms.   . . . . .

David sat in the middle of the group of twelve children who were sitting on the floor near the piano. He sat with his elbows on his knees, his hands under his chin holding up his head, and what seemed like a bored expression on his face. He neither smiled nor spoke. The children sang the turkey song but David's expression did not change. Neither did he open his mouth. The children were then turkeys, but David sat, his arms wrapped around his legs. The duckling song came next. David did not sing, but he did crawl hesitantly under the table after another child when the song was acted out. Two other songs followed, but David just sat, saying nothing, not singing.

. . . . .

Benny started to beat on his drum vigorously as soon as he got it. He half clenched his teeth and had an aggressive gleeful look on his face. He stamped his feet alternately as he beat. The teacher began to play a simple rhythm on the piano with a slow regular beat. Benny picked up the rhythm almost immediately, keeping in time but seeming to have a hard time holding himself down to the slow rhythm; a determined smile was on his face.

The next rhythm was faster and he got away from the time completely, beating madly on the drum as rapidly as he could. The teacher suggested that they have a parade. Benny joined in enthusiastically, walking around beating wildly as the line was becoming organized. When the teacher asked for quiet, Benny said very vigorously, "Shhhhh!" As the parade started, he was at the end of the single line. He ran ahead for a moment and got in front, but almost immediately he circled around and got back at the end, following along beating time and marching with vigorous stamping steps in time with his beating. In a moment the parade speeded up. Benny speeded up even faster than the others, stamping, then running; he had a grim aggressive smile on his face, and his teeth were clenched. The parade broke up in general chaos, Benny joining the others in beating madly on his drum. The teacher then started a very slow rhythm. Benny kept in rhythm with the piano most of the time, but occasionally broke loose and put in three or four extra very vigorous beats. He looked up and watched the teacher intently as she played, swaying his body in time; then he joined another mad drumming as all the children made as much noise as they could and the rhythm broke up. During this noise the teacher started again to play slowly and Benny tried to get into rhythm with her, even though many of the other children were still beating madly and paying no attention to the piano.*

* From Ruth E. Hartley, Lawrence K. Frank, and Robert M. Goldenson, *Understanding Children's Play*, pp. 311–12. New York: Columbia University Press, 1952. By permission of the publisher.

9

BY-PRODUCTS OF THE DAILY RECORDS

DETAILED and accurate recording of behavior furnishes a teacher with much more information about a child than she started out to look for. Such things as intellectual development, physical style and growth, or even adjustment to school can be drawn out of the record and summarized. The behavior of a child is an integrated thing, and poor functioning in one aspect of behavior (e.g., emotional) almost certainly affects behavior in others (e.g., intellectual, physical).

Intellectual Development

In pulling out details that indicate the intellectual functioning of a child, we must proceed from the realization that there is disagreement among psychologists and educators as to what intelligence actually is, whether it can be measured, what influences it, etc. Teachers do well, therefore, to look at a child's intellectual development as at other aspects of growth—i.e., ongoing, changing, interacting, responding, and dynamic—unless there is serious illness or severe deprivation. This is more profitable than trying to *measure* intelligence in young children.

INTELLECTUAL PICTURE

How does a child use language (in relation to his age)?
Vocabulary—meager, adequate, rich, etc.
Sentence structure—simple, complex, inaccurate
Ability to relate comprehensible story
Is the sequence logical?
Does the standpoint from which the child tells the story remain consistent or does it change?
Does he wander into bypaths of unrelated items?
Is he distracted by others?
Originality, creativity with words and ideas

74

(Evidence for the above could come also from a child's stories, conversations, and participation in discussion.)

Knowledge of the world

Does he have information about mechanical processes, natural processes, animals, social processes and relations, etc.?

How accurate or confused is his information, as evidenced in conversation, discussion, dramatic play?

In dramatic play, how well does he understand the function of the role he takes?

Does he recognize animate and inanimate objects, and pictures of them? Does he know the difference between real and make-believe?

How does he show his information?

(through play, through stories, on trips, through talking, through experiences like cooking, science experiments, etc.)

Abstract concepts

Orientation in time and space

(days of the week, time in relation to arrival and departure, seasons, age, direction, etc.)

Ability to generalize and deduce (reasoning)

Mathematical concepts—which ones does he seem to have?

(half in relation to whole, number of fingers on hand, number of children in group, simple practical addition and subtraction, etc.)

Seeing relationships (parts to each other, parts to the whole)

Evidence for the above is readily found in discussions, conversation, and varied daily experiences (counting children and things, recognition of time for routine, block-building, dramatic play, science experiments, use of puzzles, etc., recognition of succession of events, making circle of chairs, etc.).

Capacity to learn

Curiosity, as evidenced by interest in materials, new experiences, trips, natural phenomena, etc.

Correlation of past experience with new

Concentration and time spent at activity or interest

Imagination in ideas and play; use of past experiences creatively

Ability to understand and carry out directions

Ability to learn from vicarious experiences (stories, etc.)

Physical Development

The child's height, weight, build, posture, frame, and coloring might be set down at any one time for an impressionistic, or final, record. However, daily activity will show such persistent aspects of functioning as the following:

Health and the secondary effects of illnesses, operations, and physical handicaps

Grace and coordination and their relation to emotional functioning

Usual tempo

Freedom or restraint of movement—expansive, abandoned, precise, vigorous, mild

Amount of energy expended in relation to activity (how quickly does he become fatigued?)

Physical "quality" of the child—poised, restless, serene, earthbound, airy, stolid

Attitude toward use of the body in relation to large muscular movements, such as running, climbing, etc. (eagerness, caution, fear, pleasure, etc.)

Attitude toward use of the body in relation to fine body movements, such as writing, sewing, etc. (relaxed, tense, enjoys, tries too hard, etc.)

Usual facial expression (frowns, smiles, looks serene, etc.)

Adjustment to School

Adjustment to school is something else that cannot be set to absolute standards and in its specifics will be different for different children. Yet we can get a general over-all picture of a child's functioning if we do not feel too rigid about standards ourselves.

We might think of a child as adjusted to school, when he comes readily without his mother, knows school routines, group rules, and normal daily procedures, knows where materials are, who people are, what is expected of him and what he may expect of others. Incidentally, early records that show the child's first responses to a new situation are helpful in assessing the changes that take place with familiarity. The "feeling" that a teacher has about a child's being well adjusted to school should be bolstered by tangible, concrete evidence that this is really so. One might see two levels of adjustments: (1) Separation from mother—reactions to routines, knowledge of where things are, etc.; and (2) when he is really himself, natural and spontaneous.

Summaries of the intellectual and physical functioning of a child, and the overview of his adjustment to school as revealed by the records, give us additional clues to use at some time in interpretation.

10

THE FINAL SUMMARY—AND INTERPRETATION

WE HAVE taken a child through his school day now for many months. We caught his expression as he arrived in the morning, we observed how he removed his outer clothes; we watched him at play, noting both his use of materials and his relationships with other children; we noticed how he conducted himself at the table, how he took care of his bodily needs, just how he responded to us and how he behaved as a member of the group. Hopefully, we learned something of what he thinks about himself as a person and how he feels he is getting along. Perhaps too, we got clues to what we could do to satisfy his particular needs for facing life now and in the future. All this material we put into the daily records, summed up in sections so as to get at it easily (Routines, Materials, Relations with Adults, Relations with Children).

Need for a Summary

There comes a time when we are interested in a final summary of the child's behavior over time. It may be for the school files and next year's teacher, it may be for consultation with the school psychologist, or it may be for a conference with the parent. In any case, we need to pull our material together in such a way that we can get a fairly complete picture of a child's behavior at school.

All the summaries dealing with certain areas of functioning (routines, materials, etc.) will indicate a child's interaction with his environment. One can see what the patterns have been and what they have become. One will see growth, or perhaps lack of growth or even regression. The importance of any given area to the child will show up—his degree of interest and intensity, and whether these led to satisfaction or frustration. His behavior can be looked at in relation to that of

77

others of his age (They all seem able to take their clothes *off*, but not put them on again!), and to coming growth (He's finally gotten to the first rung of the jungle gym; he'll surely get to the top in the coming months). But conclusions must remain tentative (I think he'll come through . . . It looks as though . . . It seems to me . . .). All the conclusions about children's behavior need to be tested through further observation, action, and still further observation. At no time can we say about a dynamic, growing human being, "Aha, I've got him!" and be sure we are right.

Features of the Final Summary

In the final summary, we include digests of the summarized patterns of behavior at routines, with materials, with children, and with adults. We include the intellectual picture, the physical picture, and perhaps the adjustment to school. We could include such observations as how he reacts to frustration, and from what he gains satisfaction. We might include also information gleaned otherwise than through observation, such as items from the admittance file, the nurse's files, or conferences with parents.

All this evidence is then looked at with fresh and creative eyes, to see which parts in one section seem to have a bearing on other parts elsewhere. For example, a summary of use of outdoor equipment (which we have not included by itself) might show a consistent picture of non-use. Is it fear? The child looks sturdy enough, but he does not hang by his legs on the hi-lo, climb to heights, slide down the high slide, etc. He plays outside with apparent contentment, but only with the wagons, the sand, chalk, balls, water, etc. Anything more than two feet high apparently is not for him. Is there anything in his play elsewhere that seems related to this behavior? Is there anything in the information on his health and physical background? Is it connected with his age? Is there anything in his choice of stories or activities in rhythms? Is there anything he said at discussion (or did not say when everyone else was clamoring to say the same thing)? Does he behave with caution everywhere? Does he show any tension in situations of height (for example, at the head of the stairs)? Does he seem generally contented? In other words, how does this piece of behavior fit in relation to whatever else we know about him? By itself, non-use of high equipment can be open to a variety of inapt interpretations, depending on the fancy of the observer. But in relation to other aspects of a child's behavior, it takes on the specific meaning it has *for this child,* and that can be anything from simple inexperience and normal caution to undeveloped muscles, malnutrition, or fear of heights.

Let us take other possible relationships. A child has certain attitudes toward other children. Is there anything in his attitude toward adults that seems to be of a piece? Is his attitude toward himself and his accomplishments with materials involved here? Does his capacity to take frustration, as evidenced in numerous situations, relate to his getting along with children?

What behavior at routines is related to behavior with adults? What behavior at play is related to behavior with adults? What behavior at the table is related to behavior with children? Is there a common thread running throughout? the same happy-go-lucky attitudes at routines, at play, and with adults? the same inability to find satisfaction? the same even keel? the same passionate outbursts, etc.?

TRENDS

The final record includes the *trends* of behavior.

. . . . .

Apparently Cy is outgrowing his need to suck his thumb. Over the months he has left off perpetual sucking for brief returns at rest hour.

. . . . .

Al stops now for a good look when someone comes toward him fast. Instead of screaming, he sizes up the situation. He turns and runs without looking back.

. . . . .

Lynn sits with books and really seems to be enjoying them. She sits through a short story too, apparently able to follow it. Last week she asked a question about the character in the story. Lynn is learning to concentrate on happenings outside herself!

. . . . .

PROBLEMS

Perhaps if we recognize that the growing-up process is not accomplished with smoothness and evenness by anyone, we can use the word *problems* in its proper context. Every child at some time or other has a problem or hurdle to overcome and conquer if he is to grow.

These problems, or hurdles, might also be indicated in the final summary.

. . . . .

Lucy has yet to learn not to cry when she is denied something she asks for. Her disappointment is so keen, whether it is over a lollipop before lunch, a doll in someone else's possession, or no place at the easel when she wants to paint, that it seems quite out of proportion to the many real satisfactions she has in her life. She has come to expect gratification for all her wants, and of course life is not like that. She is generally a happy child and really enjoys herself immensely at school. But it is important that she learn to accept frustration with somewhat better grace. This is true more for her own sake than for her relationships with children. The children like her and play with her. But she makes herself unhappy unnecessarily.

. . . . .

EVALUATING GROWTH

The trends and problems merge into an evaluation of growth. "He has grown so much" has real meaning when it is qualified: He has learned to . . . . . . ; he used to . . . . . . , but now . . . . . . ; . . . . . . he uses so many colors, so many materials, so many ideas and words; he makes, he says, he does. It is all in the record. And how easily we forget what children did three months ago if we do not write it down!

PROGNOSIS

We can guess at what the future holds for a child's growth and can recommend what he should have for the best chances for growth. We can make recommendations to his next teacher and perhaps to his parents.

. . . . .

The record shows that he has just begun to take an interest in classroom responsibilities. He should have a chance to continue this experience and gain satisfaction from it. He is not yet ready to take on responsibility without adult help, and he should not be expected to do so for a while. But if it can be doled out to him at his pace, he will surely grow into independent responsibility too.

. . . . .

Kathy will probably sail through next year like a charm. Although her adjustment to school was somewhat stormy for a while (she cried when her mother left, she clung to the teacher, she attacked anyone who touched her clay, her puzzle, her doll, etc.), she has come to feel so at home that one would not know it was the same child. She plays with two other children (Margery and Theresa) who will go on with her next year. She uses materials with creative pleasure. She is relaxed with the teacher and has visited in next year's classroom several times. The worst seems to be over, and she should be able to get real satisfaction from her new group from the very beginning. My guess is that if there is an initial readjustment again (which is possible) she will get over it comparatively easily.

. . . . .

EXTREMES

In the final record we would note *extremes* of behavior, such as overdependence, over-all immaturity with materials, complete rejection of routines or over-all extraordinary competence. Every child can be expected to show some inconsistency, but extremes of behavior may mean real trouble or special talent and should be noted. Along the same lines are such special problems as stuttering, excessive thumb-sucking, accident-proneness, nail-biting, etc. These behaviorisms are normal to young children but cause us concern when they take up so much of a child's energy that there is little left for wholesome play.

THE WHOLE CHILD

We must also note the special quality of the personality as we see it—dramatic, charming, gentle, sturdy, slithery, bright, etc.—the first thing we think of as we think about a child, the over-allness of him. After recording minutiae, we have the right to give our own sensory impression! Not every child calls forth the one apt word. But many do, and we need not hesitate to include it in the final summary. We may well begin or end a summary of a child's behavior with "He is an imp," "She is all daintiness," "He is manly," "She is an utterly competent person," etc. On their own, these words and phrases are open to question. But with evidence piled up in the summary of many aspects of behavior, the teacher is justified in adding this wholly understandable personal touch.

Interpretation

By this time we seem to know our child well. There does not seem to be a trick we have missed. The next question we ask of his behavior

is WHY? Why does he do as he does? Is it because he was "spoiled"?
Is it because of a loving or rejecting mother, grandmother, brother, or
sister? Is it because he feels inadequate, overconfident? Is it
. . . . . . ? Is it . . . . . . ? Of course we want to know. We work
with the child, and do things for and with him. It is impossible not
to form conclusions as to the causes of his behavior.

Whether we are right or wrong can make all the difference in the
world to a child's growth and happiness. It is dangerous to interpret
incorrectly. Any interpretation at all not only must be tentative and
subject to change if new facts emerge, but must relate to a background of information which is indispensable.

WHAT TEACHERS NEED TO KNOW TO UNDERSTAND THE CAUSES OF A CHILD'S BEHAVIOR

The physical side of behavior
>   Do we know what is a well or ill child?
>   Do we know the effects of illness on a child? the effects of
>   malnutrition on a child?
>   Are we sure that a timely piece of bread and butter won't be as
>   effective as a hug? or vice versa?
>   And do we understand the relation between physical state and
>   emotional? between physical and intellectual?

Facts about child development
>   How do children grow in our culture?
>   Are there stages?
>   Is there an orderly progression? Is it the same for everyone?
>   Can we have reasonable expectations about a child's behavior
>   at any given age? What determines these?
>   Is temperament real? Is there a pace and a pattern growth for
>   each child?
>   Is personality inherited?

Cultural influences on personality and growth
>   Does every neighborhood place a premium on the same kind of
>   behavior?
>   Does every family conform to neighborhood expectations?
>   Do national standards and values play a part in parent and child
>   behavior?

Individual experience
>   Do we know the specific events that have affected this particular
>   child?
>   Have his life stresses been identical with anyone else's?

What kinds of people have shaped him and given him his views of the world?

Interpretation is difficult because it involves knowing so much. It involves feelings too, *our* feelings. Can we put ourselves in a child's place? Can we do it and remain objectively adult? Or do we respond to what we like or don't like, agree with or disagree with, as we interpret? Are we competing with the parents when we find fault with the child? Are we boosting our own morale when we say he has made superior progress?

Interpreting causes of behavior is dangerous unless we tread carefully. Can we verify every statement we make? Do we have evidence for our hunches and our guesses? Is the child more important to us than being right? Are we willing to give up a pet theory because it really does not fit the child?

The same behavior can mean different things in different children. Children hit out of anger, fear, resentment, jealousy, panic, and defiance. They can withdraw into silence out of anger, fear, resentment, jealousy, panic, and defiance. A child will not necessarily do what we do, although some will. We must learn to study children in general and find the answers for the individual child about whom we are concerned. We must study individuals and extend our understanding to all. Each human being is unique, as we ourselves are. Each human being wants to be understood for himself, as we ourselves do. Let us be just to the children we teach, and guard their precious individualities. If we would understand them, let us learn to gather accurately the evidence that will give us the clues we need. To our clues we must bring the illumination offered by knowledge of human behavior.

The following is a final summary prepared at the end of the school year by one little boy's teacher.

Final Summary—Lee M., age 4 yrs. 5 mo.

Lee has accomplished much in his adjustment to school. His first days at school were quite unhappy. He was reluctant to leave home and mother and registered his disapproval in no uncertain terms. His favorite quote seemed to be "My mother says I don't have to do that." Now he rarely mentions his family and is only occasionally anxious to take some of his work home. He still brings possessions from home to show, or share with us. Other than these material bridges between home and school, we hear very little about Lee's life away from school.

Upon entering school Lee resisted vigorously any and all routines, gradually accepting them one by one. He has never had a toilet accident at school, but called for the utmost privacy in toileting, and usually postponed the process until he reached home. It was not until December that he went willingly without signs of stress. I was delighted last week to have him come to me and say, "You know, I went to the bathroom twice already." He knows when we wash hands, and washes his in methodical fashion. He eats his snack matter-of-factly, placing cup and napkin in wastebasket when finished. He rests quietly after settling down on his rug. He dresses and undresses himself, asking for help only when necessary. He knows where to hang his clothes, and is careful to hang them up correctly.

Lee's work with creative materials has been largely teacher-initiated. Before he begins any activity he usually spends some time watching the other children. Then when he apparently feels more sure of himself he begins. His attention span is adequate to complete the activity. He works deliberately and quietly, absorbed and interested in the task at hand. It is quite evident that this is real work. His work is neat and carefully done. When he abandons this approach to materials, he seems worried, and seeks reassurance from the teacher that his untidiness is accepted comfortably by her. He verbalizes as he works, a running commentary to teacher, children, or no one. He shows pride in accomplishment and again often seeks approval from the teacher. His work with clay is delightful and imaginative and he seems to feel more freedom here than in the use of other media. Considering Lee's relationships with the teachers, he is an extremely articulate child who makes his wants known easily and often—in case of emergency, with loud calls for help. He finds it easy to verbalize his feelings in many cases, and he also reveals the intensity of these feelings. In everything he does we can see a real need for love and approval from the teacher, and an undercurrent of worry that she may possibly disapprove of his behavior.

With his peers Lee shows a pattern of caution, observing them closely before he joins them. It has just been during the past few weeks that he has taken part in singing and rhythmic group activities. He seems to derive great satisfaction from this type of activity, asking, "Are we going to play the Jingle Bell game today?" etc. If sufficiently absorbed in a certain task he ignores others in his immediate vicinity completely. He is friendly with most children, but tends to seek out one particular child to play with. This child changes on a day-to-day or week-to-week basis. When a third child enters (in my notes, it seems always Michael) he feels very insecure, covering his feelings of hostility with a sulky withdrawal, seldom with an overt act of aggression. (This week I did see him pounce unexpectedly upon Michael's back and wrestle him to the floor with triumphant laughter on his part and complete bewilderment on Michael's.) Although Lee talks a great deal he seems to be talking *at* the children most times, not *with* them. They all delight in listening to his tall stories. He has a good sense of humor and his hearty laugh can be heard throughout the room. He often uses laughter as a release from tension.

Lee seems well able to think things through. He has good ideas and definite concepts of the world about him (size, time, etc.) although sometimes these emerge in his conversation in a slightly garbled form (e.g., While attempting to crawl from the top of one packing case to another about two and one half feet away, he looked around for a plank to bridge the gap. Seeing none, he surveyed his prone figure solemnly, and then said in resigned tones, "I need more long. . . .")

When he is happy, Lee is happy from head to toe. His eyes dance, he roars with laughter, and quivers with delight. He sparkles long after the experience has ended, and seems to be reliving the pleasure he found. He is evidently able to absorb quite a few hard knocks physically—I have only one notation of his being hurt and crying. His cautious approach to life may partly account for this. When fearful or anxious he quickly seeks security in contact with the teacher. Certain defensive techniques have been noted during the year. As I have mentioned, he quoted his mother constantly in his first days at school. Also, he used such alibis as "I'm tired," or "It's too noisy," especially when making up his mind to conquer a certain task confronting him. Then too, he creates choices for himself as a face-saving gesture (e.g., "I'll rest, but I won't eat my cooky"). Just lately he has shown signs of an approaching readiness to take aggressive action (e.g., wrestling with Michael and Paul). His mother says that he reported proudly at home, "I had a big fight and I made that kid almost cry." Actually it was a very little fight, but its importance to Lee in his self-picture is very evident, for here is a child who *never* will tell anything at all about school to his mother. However, Lee will still need a great deal of encouragement to face up to his difficulties.

Lee finds great satisfaction in measuring up to what is expected of him. This is very noticeable in routines where he now accepts his weaknesses as a matter of course. The other day he, in turn, reassured Bobby, who needed help with a zipper, "Everybody needs help. Everybody but mommies, daddies, and teachers."

SUGGESTIONS FOR FURTHER READING

AMERICAN COUNCIL ON EDUCATION, Commission on Teacher Education. *Helping Teachers Understand Children.* Washington, D. C.: The Council, 1945. 468 p.

ANDERSON, J. E. "Methods of Child Psychology," in Leonard Carmichael, Ed., *Manual of Child Psychology.* Pp. 1–59. New York: John Wiley & Sons, Inc., 1946. 1068 p.

BARKER, R. G., AND WRIGHT, H. F. *One Boy's Day: A Specimen Record of Behavior.* New York: Harper and Brothers, 1951. 435 p.

BARKER, R. G., AND WRIGHT, H. F. *The Mid-West and Its Children.* Evanston, Ill.: Row, Peterson & Company, 1955.

BIBER, B., MURPHY, LOIS, AND OTHERS. *Child Life in School: A Study of a Seven-Year-Old Group.* Pp. 48–54. New York: E. P. Dutton & Co., Inc., 1942. 658 p.

FRANK, L. K. "Projective Methods for the Study of Personality." *Journal of Psychology,* 8, pp. 389–413, 1939.

HARTLEY, R. E., FRANK, L. K., AND GOLDENSON, R. M. *Understanding Children's Play.* Pp. 341–45. New York: Columbia University Press, 1952. 372 p.

HOROWITZ, R., AND MURPHY, L. B. "Projective Methods in the Psychological Study of Young Children." *Journal of Experimental Education,* 7, pp. 133–40, 1938.

LERNER, E., AND MURPHY, L. B. *Methods for the Study of Personality in Young Children.* Monograph of the Society for Research in Child Development, VI, p. 30, 1941.

MURPHY, L. B. *Personality in Young Children.* New York: Basic Books, 1956. 2 vol.

PELLER, LILLI. "Significant Symptoms in the Behavior of Young Children." *Mental Hygiene,* 30, pp. 285–95, 1946.

STONE, L. J., AND CHURCH, J. *Childhood and Adolescence.* Pp. 386–412. New York: Random House, Inc., 1958. 456 p.